SOCIAL SCIENCE AND SOCIAL WORK

Applications of Social Science in the Helping Professions

by

JEAN R. PEARMAN

The Scarecrow Press, Inc.

Metuchen, N. J.   1973

Library of Congress Cataloging in Publication Data

Pearman, Jean Richardson, 1915-
    Social science & social work.

        1. Social service--Addresses, essays, lectures.
    2. Social sciences--Addresses, essays, lectures.
    I. Title.
    HV37.P4   361'.008   73-8647
    ISBN 0-8108-0656-8

98895

PREFACE

This book is a product of a shared concern over the problem of increasing the use of knowledge generated by social scientists in achieving a more effective level of social work practice. Two major avenues for improvement exist: (1) there is great potential for more efficient use of social science knowledge in generalist or casework, group work, and community organization practice; (2) systems improvements which are essential to practice effectiveness require much social science knowledge in describing problems, determining the components of existing systems, setting policy goals and operating objectives, and arriving at new or restructured programs which can be evaluated in terms of criteria related to the established objectives. All helping services have similar problems in the utilization of social science content.

The helping professions are responding to rapid technological and social changes. This book, which is an expression of long and anxious concern over professional inadequacies, was motivated by the following current developments.

1. A movement away from a strong emphasis on individual rehabilitation to more developmental and preventive approaches to helping, to the extent that social science is becoming more important to helping service methodologies.

2. A growing professional interest in a merged client-social systems approach to direct and indirect practice.

3. A mutual need among teachers and practitioners to effectively employ social science knowledge and techniques to measure accountability in social work, education, urban planning, public health, guidance counseling and other helping professions.

4. The trend toward merging graduate and undergraduate curricula in social work into a continuum, usually with a social systems focus.

5. The development of schools of applied social science and schools of helping services.

6. The rapid growth of information and referral services which need a strong descriptive and theoretical knowledge of all social systems and the systems approach to service and program organization.

The co-authors of eight of the chapters contained in this book deserve more recognition than the acknowledgement of their co-authorship by chapter. In many instances, they have offered suggestions related to other chapters. Special recognition is due Dr. William T. Olson of the Florida State University Department of Urban and Regional Planning for his instruction on systems analysis. In addition to our own experiences, education, and research, the authors have drawn from the works of outstanding social scientists and helping services educators. Discussions with students and colleagues have stimulated discoveries which have contributed to content.

Special thanks are due Patricia Ann Terrie, Patti Rose, and Patricia Pearman, who typed most of the manuscript.

J. R. Pearman, Ph. D. , ACSW
Professor of Social Work
School of Social Welfare
Florida State University
Tallahassee, Florida

CONTENTS

Page

TABLES

Page

FIGURES

FOREWORD

The helping professions have long been concerned with improving the quality and scope of their performance. At the same time, their methods of evaluating and measuring "quality" have come under criticism. The values and goals of the helping professions have also been under review as recent attacks have mounted on the "services strategy" in meeting human needs.

My own role over the past forty years has been primarily in applying the "incremental" approach in the legislative formulation or administrative implementation of social policy. I have encountered many different theories of human motivation and values in my efforts to obtain the enactment of social legislation. I have tended to find that most legislators, the public, and publicists use "theories" to justify their preconceived conclusions. The clash of theories in the legislative domain is usually decided not by the demonstrated validity of the respective theories, but usually by the "conventional wisdom" of the body politic through the elected representatives of the people.

This does not mean that social science theory is not used, respected, or of help in practical situations. It is one of the tools used by the protagonists in the battle of ideas, ideals, and programs.

My eight years of experience in the formulation and administration of programs in the Department of Health, Education, and Welfare during 1961-69 convince me that we need more emphasis on the contribution which social science theory can make to social policy.

There is a great and growing surge of interest in improving the "delivery systems" in health, education, law enforcement, welfare, the postal system, etc. The developing support for basic changes in these delivery systems means basic changes in professional responsibilities, in the power structure of the professions, and in the role of

ix

consumer-professional relationships.

I believe that by 1976--the 200th anniversary of the Declaration of Independence--we will be making new commitments in social policy for the future. Social science theory must help in this long-range effort.

Wilbur J. Cohen

Wilbur J. Cohen

Secretary of Health, Education
and Welfare, 1968

Dean, School of Education,
The University of
Michigan, 1969-

1. INTRODUCTION: THE FUNCTION OF SOCIAL SCIENCE IN THE HELPING SERVICES

Defining, learning and applying truths are elusive and difficult tasks. Facts may be learned, but these facts are not easily convertible into reliable truths. Concepts and principles may form guidelines for practitioners, but the test of time may reveal ineffectiveness. Perhaps the Hegelian viewpoint of a thesis and contervailing anti-thesis interacting to produce a higher level of synthesis, or truth, is the best way to view knowledge in theoretical and applied social science under existing levels of development. It is hard to distinguish between a belief based on little or no fact and a plausible but not totally reliable concept, based on sufficient empirical data to justify a hypothetical statement arrived at inductively, or a generalization reached through the logical application of a carefully tested premise, deductively. Also, it is hard to discern the degree of refinement in one of a sequence of hypotheses which may lead progressively toward truth. But a cop-out on an irrelevance plea is more suicidal than positive if one is interested in the perpetuity of homo sapiens.

Two general approaches may be used to bring helpful social science concepts to the helping services. One approach is to require at least a token sampling of the social sciences in the educational requirements for helping service training. On the surface, this policy seems appropriate and dynamic. Conceivably, the lag in the application of new social science concepts might be reduced and, if the student can accomplish adequate synthesis, time may be saved for teaching professional skills and attitudes. But if social science faculty do not thoroughly understand the relationships of their disciplines to the helping professions, and if the faculty teaching the helping methods cannot see the relevance of theoretical and descriptive social science knowledge to professional skills and attitudes, then the most enterprising and intelligent student may become discouraged. And the impression of irrelevancy may increase if agency personnel cannot help the graduate to apply a rapidly evaporating store of significant social science knowledge. Another model,

1

which is somewhat more systemic than the first suggestion,
would feed in partially synthesized social science concepts.
This approach is intriguing, but it calls for students with a
base of fundamental principles in the social sciences and
alert, aggressive helping service instructors with an eager-
ness to transfer useful social science knowledge into practice. Because of several barriers, which will receive later
discussion, neither model has been generally effective.

Commonalities in Social Science and Helping Service Concepts

If the semantics barrier can be broken, similar concepts can be found among the social science and helping service disciplines. But intra-house as well as interdisciplinary
confusion exists. For example, opinions as to the potential
for subsystem manipulation vary with viewpoints as to the
nature of social organization and the total systemic configura-
tion. If we take the classical or eighteenth century view of
the individual and society, manipulation of the individual for
social change is absolutely essential because groups and organizations are seen as simple arithmetic sums of the behavior of individuals, in contrast with the sociological view
that groups generate their own unique characteristics. And
so it follows that social change, under the second viewpoint,
can be effected through group processes as well as through
restructuring personality systems. Or, in a helping service
application of the first, or atomistic viewpoint, the orthodox
Freudian might view society and culture as a reality situation
in which the id-ego-superego paradigm is manipulatable in
the direction of equilibrium. The constraints of society are
not viewed as an arena where the social worker or psychia-
trist or guidance worker may interfere. Similar dichotomies
in opposing views of society may be described as functional
vs mechanistic, equilibrium vs conflict theories of change,
holism vs structural-functionalism, or other concepts which
polarize as to whether total societal systems are in unitary
relationships or whether they are compartmentalized, like
some TV sets, so that parts can be repaired or improved
so as to improve the operation of the whole. Such polarization may well be illogical, since both comprehensive and
selective changes may prove to be beneficial, but such
fundamental academic and professional debates produce great
confusion, and simplistic explanations presented in a friendly, warm and seductive manner may produce loyal, but, possibly, seriously misinformed converts. The thalamus en-
cephalon frequently gets more exercise than the cortex in
the learning process and this pitfall is serious; re-education

is a central role of all helping professions.

In addition to a common interest in education, there are many common concepts with semantic variations which exist among the social sciences and the helping professions. Values, such as those related to social justice, personal freedom, materialism, or loyalty to a god, a country, a consanguine or socially-conceived family, are discussed throughout theoretical and applied social science disciplines. Social and technological change, development, anomie and alienation, marginality, maximization in the use of personal and social resources, individual and social pathologies, among other central themes, provide common threads among the social sciences and helping methodologies.

Basic Functions of Social Systems

Social systems have evolved to meet human needs, though it might be more accurate to say that some systems have been designed to meet needs of select groups or, at least, that social systems meet the needs of human beings in varying degrees. It is only in a general sense that we may say that social systems represent a flow of activities through structures to meet human needs. For example, our theoretical capitalistic economic system makes no direct provision for those who can not function effectively in the labor, capital, management or resource markets, and only limited provision for those of low productivity. Other systems, including the family system and public welfare, have compensated for this gap in a limited degree through income transfers and service programs, but it is becoming increasingly apparent that those who are most in need receive the least help. Consequently, current interest is shifting away from the once dominant restorative focus of the helping services and toward a more developmental and preventive approach through improved utilization or through structural and functional changes in social systems. Social scientists have a significant role in providing problem description, in providing knowledge essential to planned change with the predictive social telesis which has been a goal of social sciences for several decades, and in developing more effective monitoring devices.

The Need for Restructuring the Helping Services

There is a strong public demand for increased

effectiveness and decreased costs in the major helping services. All levels of education, law enforcement, health
service delivery, and welfare are among the many systems
which are facing a demand for improved accountability. It
has been suggested that needs and problems be reassessed to
the extent of developing social indicators similar to the ac-
counts which describe the performance of the economic system. Somewhat limited, but probably sufficient, information exists to permit movement toward restructuring of helping services in a developmental role-task model which would
consider current needs and change performance roles of
agency personnel or reassign roles to personnel in other
agencies where the changes can be effected. A major
problem exists in the multiple causes related to unmet needs.
Singular efforts to improve one system--for example, edu-
cation--when other related systems, such as welfare, employment, health and transportation are obviously faulty, have
usually met with little success in the achievement of objectives.

     In the re-structuring of social systems, helping ser-
vice roles must be carefully defined and related to the
knowledge, values, attitudes, and skills necessary for the
effective performance of these roles. It is largely the
strength of such work roles and related tasks which determines system effectiveness if structure permits meeting
the needs of people affected under the system. Manpower
strength is important in the production of goods despite
great capital accumulations. Manpower is all-important in
the production of services, where the impact of capital is
growing but still of lesser importance.

Contributions of Social Science in the
the Revamping of Helping Services

     The function of social science in the systems-roles-
knowledge paradigm should be readily apparent. Social science concerns the functioning of social systems which comprise the causal arenas of social and personal problems.
Theoretical and applied social science provide the means
through which the needs of both majorities and minorities
can be reconciled and met effectively. We have the material resources to accomplish the task if we choose to make
more efficient use of human and material resources.
Knowledge is a major energizer of human resources. Social
science concerns itself with systems and solutions to human
problems. Potential social science contributions include:

1. Further improvement of information on such problems as inadequate income, health, aging, employment and crime; and the generation of theoretical concepts which will guide us toward a solution of these problems.

2. The provision of more adequate descriptive and analytical data as to the helping service systems which are designed to prevent or ameliorate problems.

3. Identification and description of constraints which limit the development of more effective systems, and assistance in the origination of change strategies which will produce improvements in meeting human needs without producing socially unacceptable costs.

4. An increase in predictive skills as to the primary and secondary impact of planned changes.

5. Improvement of evaluative systems in relation to the fulfillment of defined objectives.

Practitioners need to know relevant systems structurally and functionally in order to provide adequate linking and coordinating services for clients among hundreds of need-related but poorly structured and loosely interrelated programs. Or, if practitioners join policy makers and planners in effecting planned change, then social science is needed for accurate perception of functional problems related to human needs and values associated with existing systems. The developing specialty of social systems analysis concerns groups or sets of entities or components, which are meaningfully interrelated and sufficiently bounded, interacting in a multidimensional field to achieve a specific purpose or purposes. Social science knowledge is essential when the system approach is applied to problems of human interaction.

The challenges in trying to improve the effective application of social science in the helping professions are great, but so is the need. All helping service workers--social workers, teachers, nurses, guidance counselors, and vocational counselors--must learn more of the structure and function of community systems and related subsystems. In addition, the concept of the interaction between personality and social systems must be strengthened. In practice, transactional effectiveness must be improved. Both prior to and following the appropriate restructuring of social service systems, helping service personnel must learn more effective teamwork in the solution of individual, group, and

community problems. The following chapters give further
explanation of the central themes related to social science
and the helping professions which have been briefly summarized here. Some suggested educational changes which
would improve the application of social science to social
work and related professions are followed by some illustra-
tions of relevance and means through which pertinent social
science concepts and related information may be selected and
integrated.

PART I

PROBLEMS AND APPROACHES TO
SOCIAL SCIENCE-SOCIAL WORK INTEGRATION

Professional social work in the United States began with a great interest in the social environment and one might wonder why we did not continue this emphasis, as has been the case in Great Britain and other northern European countries. Certainly, the community organization societies, Jane Addams and her colleagues in Hull House, and Mary Richmond in Social Diagnosis were aware of and concerned about the interaction of individuals and social systems in their efforts to meet needs, and they actively sought social change. The Freudian input, beginning in the 1920s, produced a professional retreat from the early focus on social environment. Now, once again, social work as well as other professional helping disciplines, including education, are moving away from such a strong emphasis on direct behavior changing. Movement is toward a dynamic conceptualization of relationships between human beings and social systems.

Part I reviews the cyclical history of educational interest in social science which was largely related to a shifting emphasis to and away from direct behavior changing, as contrasted with a more balanced approach which included planned system change. Barriers to the integration of social science into social work, even in a period of strong demand for such content, are summarized.

Role shifts are related to social change and changing systems. Objectives of social work education are related to course content in terms of emerging roles and the knowledge, skills, values and attitudes needed for the effective performance of these roles. As a client-social system

7

approach is gaining fuller acceptance, attention is given to means of gaining more effective integration of social science into social work and related helping professions.

Lastly, some common concepts of social science, social welfare and social work are recognized, the impact of polarization of viewpoints as to the basic nature of society and social systems, and some negatives of chauvinism as to professional or disciplinary affiliation are indicated. A more global viewpoint of social welfare and quality of life is suggested for social work and other related helping services.

2. THE SOCIAL AND BEHAVIORAL SCIENCE INPUT TO SOCIAL WORK PRACTICE*

The importance of social science in social work education has been widely acclaimed. Some proven gains have been made through the borrowing and adaptation of social science concepts and theory--especially from the areas of social psychology, anthropology, and sociology. Two decades ago, Stanley Davis joined with such loyal advocates as Gordon Hamilton and Eveline Burns in a post-World War II revival of interest in putting the social back into social work. He thought that knowledge of all of man's social relations could be an advantage to social work practice. In his opinion, the more fully social work used social science to evaluate the facts behind its espoused causes, measured the results of the functions which it performed and tested those assumptions repeatedly, the more social work would contribute to human welfare. He also held that social work had an obligation to make its own contributions toward a more effective interdisciplinary science of human relations (Davis, 1951).

But the incorporation of social science theory and factual content into social work education has been a difficult task, especially in the areas of economics and political science. The history of this stormy affair, with frequent separations and rather dissatisfying reconciliations, has been tacitly recognised. We have been reluctant to accept divorce on the grounds of basic incompatibility, but, at times, frustrations were sufficiently great to bring us close to that point. Now we seem to have a very active interest in increasing the effectiveness of social work through wider and deeper inputs from the social sciences. This suggests recognition of the social values-social science theory-social systems-accountability paradigm in social organisation.

---

*Reproduced by permission of the co-author, Barbara Jean Stewart, B. S. W. , M. S. Sc.

Consequently, it seems appropriate to re-examine the past
with the goal of finding pitfalls and troublesome barriers
which may be removed so that current efforts will be an
even greater success than was the case during other periods
of high interest.

The Cyclical History of Social Science-
Social Work Integration Rates

Briefly, the swing has been from a general interest
in the social system to a focus on the personality system of
the client and back to a more pronounced interest in the social system. In the early years of social work, 1892-1917,
Mary Richmond and others emphasized social legislation, reform of institutions, and problem prevention. In fact, social
work was one of the roots of social science, as sociology
and economics had their origins in reform and problem-
solving interests. From a harmonious childhood, we drifted
apart as social science sought truth in highly abstracted
theories, and social work, obsessed with the Freudian input
of the 1920s, sought an integrated, non-eclectic approach in
the restoration of deviants to acceptable social functioning.
Individual pathology as the basic cause of maladjustment became suspect in the 1930s as the failures of the social system became apparent to the observant professional. Social
work was shaken by the diagnostic-functional rift as immediate experiences and perception of reality became more important than the subconscious and early developmental trauma
to many practitioners in the field of social welfare. World
War II and its immediate aftermath brought partial rein-
statement of some of the previous emphasis on individual
restoration, the one-to-one approach and salvation through
direct efforts to improve mental health. But gradually, we
turned back toward the improved understanding and manipulation of environmental forces. The community mental health
concept involving a team approach from an increasing number of related helping disciplines gained acceptance. The
1950s brought a very strong interest in the incorporation of
social science content into social work methods. After a
period of complacence in the late 1950s and early 1960s,
poverty, riots, pollution, and a number of other group problems brought macro-solutions into a renewed and continuing
emphasis. Cyclical changes in social science utilization were
reviewed by Chambers (1962), Siporin (1970), and Borenzweig
(1971). The unanswered question is: "Where are we going
with the social science input this time?"

Recent Social Science-Social Work Integration Efforts

The emphasis of this chapter is on the past two decades. The relevancy of social science in both the theoretical and applied arenas can hardly be questioned. Both
scholars and technicians are interested in the freedom of intellectual inquiry. Theory is needed in the development of
viable methods and the practitioner may provide a testing
ground and help generate empirical data for use in the further refinement of theory. The social science-social work
schism occurred when the purist scholar disregarded relevance to existing problems and when the helping service
professional defined problems too narrowly. Compartmentalization of research and the development of specialized
models and related symbols have formed a screen to effective communication, to the growth of interdisciplinary theory, and to the development of practice-related models conducive to effective problem-solving activity (Lynd, 1939).
These historic problems have been only partially removed.
The challenge is to further reduce the barriers and utilize
content from all of the social sciences in an effort to increase the effectiveness of social work.

The 1950s

Integration of social science into social work practice
was a very serious educational objective between 1950 and
1959. Coyle (1952 and 1958), Boehm (1951), Maas (1950),
Kahn-Kadushin (1959), Pollak (1951, 1952 and 1956), Greenwood (1955), Stein (1955 and 1958), and the staff of the
Council on Social Work Education (1953), were among the
major contributors. Grace Coyle prepared a chart in Social
Science In The Professional Education of Social Workers
which illustrated the interrelationships of social sciences,
social work, and related service professions.

As the Freudian orientation spread to the social sciences, it seemed that a common ground might be established
in the relationship between social science and social work.
Elements of incompatibility over-rode this common interest.
Most importantly, case observation was not an adequate research base for social science, and social workers lacked
the knowledge essential to use social science research approaches effectively. Ernest Greenwood (1955) presented
the differences between social science and social work which
lead to difficulties in effecting maximal productive

relationships. His viewpoint may be summarized in the following manner.

Social science is an attempt to describe the characteristics and products of human behavior as they occur within
social configurations. All of the allied disciplines which
compose the social sciences study the same general materials from different points of view, with concepts, such as
competition, receiving various definitions. These descriptive propositions possess a generalizing character, and the
foremost aim or goal of social scientists is to discover,
under the surface of diversity, the thread of uniformity
which is presented by this material. Once this strand has
been isolated, the social scientist can construct a logical
class. Then, a descriptive generalization is prepared about
the class and its observed pattern and, next, the social
scientist attempts to interlock comparable classes into a
broader class to formulate a wider and more abstract generalization. The system of interlocking related propositions,
which is thereby constructed, leads to a body of theory of
the particular discipline of focus. (The mathematical input
of modern economics provides some variation in the direction of the physical sciences.)

The function of research on social science is to test
the accuracy of the theoretical models constructed through a
process which has logical and technical components. The
logical part comes first, and this consists of moving from
the theoretical models or formulations to be validated to the
hypothesis concerning the operational characteristic to be
tested. The social scientist must then translate his theoretical model from theory to an operational statement which
can be tested and either validated or invalidated. The technical aspect of the process comprises the construction of a
study design to fit the hypothesis. Once the design or plan
of action is completed, the social scientist will move through
the steps indicated in the design. Then, the degree of consistency between the theoretical formulation and the research
results is determined.

As a comparison, social work is primarily concerned
with action and change. The social scientist aims at an accurate description of social work or other social phenomena,
and control is secondary. The social work practitioner aims
at the client system, and to some extent at social system
control, and knowledge may be subordinated to this objective.
Essentially, social science presents the laws of behavior,

while the profession of social work focuses on principles of control.

The numerous analytical efforts of the 1950s should, seemingly, have been productive of an even greater burst of published material in the 1960s.   Such high level activity might have logically led to a very rapid construction of bridging models from social science to social work.   But the developments of the next decade were rather surprising.

The 1960s

Social work literature contains very little on the facilitation of the social science theory to social work practice transfers during the first half of the decade.   But poverty and other massive social problems heightened interest.   The Council on Social Work Education issued a Curriculum for the Master's Degree Statement which gave more specific mention to social science input than had previously been the case.   There were some articles, such as those by Gyarfas (1969) and Warren (1967), which recognize the shift toward the social systems approach and the MSW becoming a "manager-programmer, " with a plea by Mary Gyarfas that some of the direct professional effort to enhance self-fulfillment and promote self-determination be retained.   Roland Warren emphasized applications of demography, systems change and community behavior.   Bloom (1969) presented a model for the incorporation of social science knowledge and suggested a specialized information retrieval team composed of both generalists and specialists.   He reiterated the barrier of social science providing for the expansion of knowledge without packaging for the systematic application of this knowledge in social work.   He suggested that strategies based on theory might prove to be more readily usable by social workers than raw theory, admitting that a conceptual gap would still remain even if a cookbook of scientifically based strategies were to be prepared.   One might be led to assume that the dearth of writing on how to transfer social science knowledge to social work practice resulted because we were in the "doing" stage rather than in the "how-to-do" stage.   This may be a partial explanation as there is some evidence of efforts to speed up the incorporation of social science theory.   Reichert (1970) concluded that social work will move further from isolation to effective incorporation of biological, behavioral science, and social science knowledge in the 1970s.

Barriers to the Incorporation of Social Science

  Literature of the past two decades is replete with suggestions as to how the social science input may aid social work. It is said that useful descriptive knowledge concerning society and the individual, such as that related to social organization, social systems and sub-systems, social class, cultures, power structure, the governing process, and economic policy, may be obtained. Theoretical knowledge concerning social problems and the interaction between the client and the social system provide useful insights. The research tools of the social sciences are recognized for their potential in making social work a more viable process. Why then, hasn't the input been greater? Several eminent social work educators have offered explanations.

  1. There is a problem of communication. (a) Social scientists have difficulty understanding each other and the gap in verbal symbols between social scientists and social workers is even greater. (b) Social science theory and substantive knowledge must be adapted for practice. (c) Seeking knowledge and effecting change are different ballgames (Boehm, 1951 and Greenwood, 1955).

  2. Distorted attitudes, unfortunate stereotyping, and the academic stratification system have reduced the quality of limited communication. A sense of urgency on the part of the social worker who is caught up in the needs of clients sometimes leads to inappropriate action. Compassion without adequate knowledge and planning may lead to ineffective or negative results. It is hard for social scientists to understand the hasty actions of social workers which sometimes seem to be on a trial and error basis (Maas, 1950). The social scientist may lose sight of humanity while the social worker may find it hard to trade-off more immediate human need attention for more research and the further development of a knowledge base.

  3. There is a necessary time lag between the generation of knowledge and effecting its practical applications (Boehm, 1951 and Kahn, 1959). This can be illustrated in the case of the systematic and highly developed theory base of economics and the political applications in the areas of public finance and monetary policies to effect solutions to problems of unemployment and greater equality in income distribution.

4.   Social science concepts vary and there is inconsistency in the meaning of basic terms.   Social work borrows
selectively, which may lead to distortions as all variables
may not be considered.   Narrow applications of social science theory and substantive knowledge may lead to some
very ineffective actions.   Also, knowledge which is generated
within a discipline is more readily acceptable than that which
is borrowed from without, even though the indigenous information may be inferior to the exogenous knowledge (Kahn-
Kadushin, 1959).

5.   The clinical model, with a concentration on behavior changing, has narrowed the potential utility of social
science in the social work processes and there is still some
latent impact of this narrow definition of social work (Borenzweig, 1971).

6.   One of the most obvious facts is that the MSW
social worker, the graduate social work student, and the
undergraduate social welfare student very frequently lack the
knowledge base for understanding and applying sophisticated
social science concepts.   Recent research concerning undergraduate social welfare educators yielded the finding that
MSW-only instructors who professed detailed knowledge of
the developmental role-task methods model were only half
as likely to test it as were the MSW+ instructors (Pearman
and Jahns, 1971).

7.   There has long been considerable resistance to
basic principles courses in the social sciences on the part
of undergraduate social welfare students.   More recently,
student actionists have demanded changes which would greatly
alter the nature of basic social systems with even less interest in textbook theoretical concepts and detailed knowledge
of social welfare sub-systems.

8.   Social science generalizations may be at a stage
of hypothesis which is short of dialectical synthesis and absolute truth.

How Can the Barriers to Social Science Be Removed?

Writers on the subject of synthesizing and integrating
content from the social sciences have made a number of
suggestions for the facilitation of this input over the past two
decades (Maas, 1950 and Greenwood, 1955).   Some of these

suggestions are:

1. Joint efforts of social workers and social scientists to develop diagnostic and treatment classifications, explore the value implications of social work theory, and explore goals.

2. The development of common course sequences for students in both social science and social work curricula, cross-fertilization through the journals, and examination of common and conflicting attitudes at joint social science-social work conferences.

3. The placing of social scientists on faculties of graduate schools of social work and the cooperation of social scientists and social workers on research projects. Research by Onken (1968) found slow development in the implementation of this recommendation, especially in the areas of economics and political science.

Other suggestions, which we favor, have had limited application.

1. In faculty building, insistence on graduate education in the social sciences as well as graduate training and experience in social work.

2. Insistence on breadth and depth in the social sciences for undergraduate welfare curriculum students and for admission to graduate schools of social work.

3. Increased emphasis on research in social work, with maximal input from the social sciences and with special attention to the evaluation of the effectiveness of social work practice. There should be increased use of computer potential in both practice and educational cost-benefit analysis. Also, research on factors which encourage or impede the trial of innovations should be furthered.

4. Re-definition of social work in terms which encompass many pertinent helping roles in addition to behavior-changing through the clinical approach.

These roles are principally evaluator, social broker, data manager, advocate and mobilizer. Figure I illustrates functional relationships between these roles and the social sciences.

Projections for the 1970s

There are factors currently existent which may sharpen interest and facilitate the process of incorporating social science concepts into social work practice.

1. Problem-solving competition is developing within the social sciences. The Committee on Problems and Policy of the Social Science Research Council, National Academy of Sciences (1969) has recommended the establishment of graduate schools of applied social and behavioral sciences which would use an interdisciplinary approach to research and the solution of social problems. An avenue for cooperative relationships may be opened in the further statement that any compatible knowledge which may be generated by discipline not directly concerned should be utilized. Schools of community services, of health and social services, and with other broad titles are being opened. Competition may produce a costly dualism, but also an opportunity for cooperation and a hint to schools of social work that they make a more effective use of social science content are present.

2. Public demand for accountability may spur efforts to make social work more effective through increased use of knowledge from the social sciences.

3. The budget demands of states and central cities upon federal public financial operations and such special problems as crime control, public health, education, population control, and pollution may restrict budgets for social work education and practice, but this multiplicity of public interest in welfare outlays may cause social work to use all available knowledge which may contribute toward increased effectiveness in social work practice.

4. Social work is accepting a systems approach which involves the integration of client and social systems. The utility of social science should, therefore, increase (Hearn, 1968).

5. The knowledge essential to effectiveness in a

Figure I
Knowledge-Practice Relationships

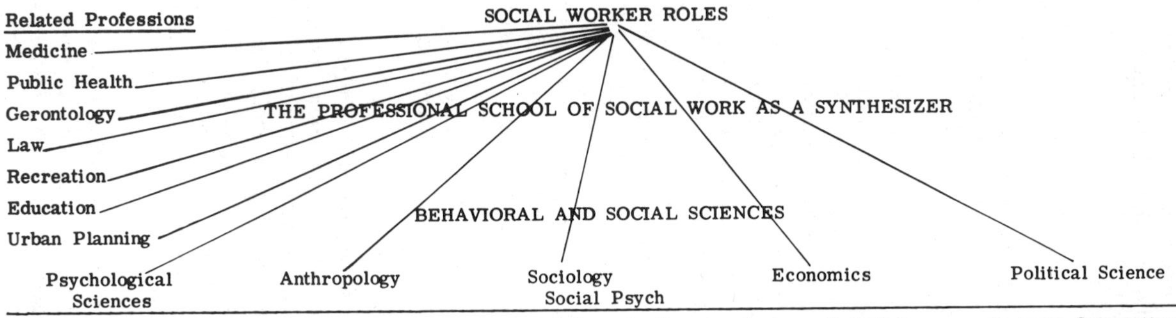

SOCIAL WORKER ROLES

THE PROFESSIONAL SCHOOL OF SOCIAL WORK AS A SYNTHESIZER

BEHAVIORAL AND SOCIAL SCIENCES

Related Professions
- Medicine
- Public Health
- Gerontology
- Law
- Recreation
- Education
- Urban Planning

Psychological Sciences	Anthropology	Sociology Social Psych	Economics	Political Science
Psychoanalytic theory	Value Concepts	Social Organization and Basic Systems	Systems Orientation	Systems Orientation
Other theory from psychiatry, e.g. reality theory	Dominant culture	Power Structure	Macro-economics and employment	Political Science Theory
Other psychological theory e.g., learning theory, operant psychology	Sub-cultures	Community Concepts	Public Finance	Compensatory policies for disadvantage in the economic system
Research Technology	Relationships to Individual Behavior Collective Behavior	Social Change Concepts including conflict theory	Monetary Theory	Political Realities
Personality Theories	Culture conflict	Demography	Welfare Theory	Relation of Public and Private Agencies
Human Growth	Research Technology	Small group theory	Distribution Theory	Check-and-balance Concept
Psychological Theory related to impact of client participation	Relationship between values and social systems	Research Technology	Cost-benefit Analysis	Techniques for Political Intervention
		Role Theory	Human Resources Investment Concepts	Research Technology
		Social Stratification	Equilibrium Concept	
			Research Technology	

growing network of information and referral agencies favor social science.

6. Perhaps one of the most effective influences may be the growing acceptance of a developmental role-task model as the integrating frame for social work methods courses. The perimeters of this broad umbrella would call for increased inputs from the social, biological, and behavioral sciences. Greater emphasis on the roles of outreach worker, social broker, advocate, evaluator, teacher, mobilizer, consultant, community planner, care giver, data manager, and administrator may make social science content more appropriate and stimulate a faster rate of adoption (Teare and McPheeters, 1970).

For example, the role of the broker would call for a knowledge of and an emotional readiness to use content concerning:

1. All basic social systems.
2. The social and economic impact of theory-based governmental policies (e.g., fiscal and monetary devices) which influence opportunities for clients.
3. Health, education and welfare sub-systems in depth.
4. The home agency of the social broker in detail.
5. Knowledge of human growth and pathological behavior.
6. Cultural differences and culture conflict.
7. Community power structure.
8. Skills which would help the client to mobilize his inner resources.
9. Skills in communicating with the client and helping techniques to facilitate a successful approach to the gatekeeper in the agency to which the client is referred.

Summary

Social science content has always been important to social work. Interest has fluctuated with change of emphasis as to the importance of social organization and social change as compared to client functioning. Restoration efforts have, at times, superseded interest in prevention and social provisioning. Differences as to the relative importance of knowledge, compassion and skill have led to variations in the emphasis placed on social science content by social work educators.

Efforts have been hampered by difficulties in communication based upon differences in purposes, variation in types and meanings of verbal symbols, and hostility related to the academic stratification system. These differences between social science and social work have, at times, been accentuated by the curriculum and personnel policies of administrators and entrenched faculties of schools and departments responsible for social work education. The public demand for a broader and more effective approach to solving the problems of society may encourage a rapid growth in social science input, but this rate will be markedly slowed if social work abandons large areas of community development and social policy determination to other educational units.

Bibliography

Bloom, M. "The selection of knowledge from other disciplines and its integration into social work curricula," J. Educ. Social Wk. 5, 15-29, 1969.

Boehm, W. W. "Social work and the social sciences," J. Psychiat. Soc. Wk. 21, 4-8, 1951.

Borenzweig, H. "Social work and psychoanalytic theory: a historical analysis," Soc. Wk. 16, 7-17, 1971.

Chambers, C. A. "An historical perspective on political action vs individualized treatment," Current Issues in Social Work Seen in Historical Perspective, New York: Council on Soc. Wk. Educ., 51-64, 1962.

Coyle, G. L. "New insights available to the social worker from the social sciences," Social Service Review 26, 289-304, 1952.

_____. Social Science in the Professional Education of Social Workers. New York: Council on Soc. Wk. Educ., 1958.

Davis, S. P. "The relationship of social science to social welfare," Soc. Wk. J. 32, 210-26, 1951.

Greenwood, E.   "Social science and social work: a theory
of their relationship, " Social Service Review 29, 20-31,
1955.

Gyarfas, M.   "Social science, technology and casework, "
Social Service Review 43, 259-72, 1969.

Hearn, G. , ed.   The General Systems Approach: Contributions Toward an Holistic Conception of Social Work, New
York: Council on Soc. Wk. Educ. , 1968.

Kahn, A. J. , ed.   Issues in American Social Work, New
York: Columbia U. Press, 1959.   See A. Kadushin,
"The knowledge base of social work, " 58-65.

Lynd, R. S.   Knowledge for What?   Princeton, N. J. :
Princeton U. Press, 1939.

Maas, H. S.   "Collaboration between social work and the
social sciences, " Soc. Wk. J. 31, 104-109, 1950.

National Academy of Sciences.   The Behavioral and Social
Sciences: Outlook and Needs, Washington, D. C. , 1969.

Onken, R.   A Survey of Faculty in Graduate Schools of Social Work.   New York: Council on Soc. Wk. Educ. ,
1968.

Pearman, J. R. and Jahns, I. R.   "The diffusion of an innovative methods model into course content"--a research
paper presented at the annual meeting of the National
Conference on Social Welfare, (1971) and accepted for publication by the Social Wk. Educ. Reporter. April-May, 1973.

Pollak, O.   Integrating Sociological and Psychoanalytic Concepts.   New York: Russell Sage Foundation, 1956.

_____.   "Relationships between social sciences and child
guidance practice, " Am. Socio. Rev. 26, 61-67, 1951.

_____, et al.   Social Science and Psychotherapy for Chil-
dren.   New York: Russell Sage Foundation, 1952.

Reichert, K.   "Current development and trends in social
work in the United States, " J. Educ. Social Wk. 6, 39-
50, 1970.

Stein, H. D.   Social Perspectives on Behavior.   Glencoe,
Ill. :   Free Press, 1958.

_____ .   "Social science and social work practice and
education, " Soc. Casework 36, 147-55, 1955.

Teare, R. J. and McPheeters, H. L.   Manpower Utilization
in Social Welfare.   Atlanta: Southern Regional Educ. Bd. ,
1970.

Warren, R. L.   "Applications of social science knowledge
in the community organization field, " J. Educ. Social
Wk. 3, 60-72, 1967.

3. AN APPROACH TO THE INTEGRATION OF RELEVANT SOCIAL SCIENCE CONTENT INTO SOCIAL WORK*

There is a growing realization that social work practice and education have been based on false premises as to the efficacy of a focus on the personality system. Therapeutic interventions which directly change behavior were thought to be: (1) extensively possible despite the constraints exerted by the broader social system; (2) effective solutions to individual and community problems within public cost limitations; (3) desirable for the client; and (4) the major substance for practitioner education. Need we re-echo the research findings as to the limitations of most methods of directly changing behavior; its ineffectiveness in problem-solving, especially among poverty clients, and the difficulty of achieving conformity to middle class and professional norms and creativity in the same time and space? Social work, which is now facing somewhat of a crisis, might well have found use for the products of a less doctrinaire and particularistic educational system for social workers. But instead of rattling skeletons, we would like to: (1) re-examine the goals of social work education; (2) relate objectives to present-day functional roles; (3) indicate knowledge essential to effective role performance; (4) describe barriers to the integration of social science content into a viable client-social systems model; and (5) suggest an approach to the removal of barriers and the facilitation of the social science integration process. Social work education must consider the public demand for solutions to problems as they are nationally defined.[1]

*This paper was presented in summary form at the 99th Annual Forum of the National Conference on Social Welfare, Chicago, May 28 - June 2, 1972. The co-author is Ann L. McLean, Assistant Professor, Graduate School of Social Work, University of Wisconsin-Madison.

Goals of Social Work Education

The primary purpose of undergraduate social work education is employment. Our study found that 463 of 675 (or 69 percent) of responding BSW alumni, agency representatives, and faculty indicated this objective. In comparison, first choice alternatives were: preparation for graduate school, 12 percent; improved citizen participation, nine percent; and "the same as any other degree," 10 percent. Since the practice entry point is now focused at the BSW level, the authors sought information as to the perceived goals and objectives of social work education by mailing questionnaires to: (1) University of Wisconsin-Madison and Florida State University undergraduate majors, 1966-71; (2) Florida and Wisconsin Social Welfare agencies; (3) all social work instructors in the Wisconsin-Madison and Florida State Universities; and (4) a random sample of social work instructors who had been concerned with undergraduate social work education throughout the United States.

Sixty-three percent of the graduates giving employment as their first choice found jobs with the BSW, as compared to 54 percent of all BSW or BSW-equivalent respondents. Fifty percent of those giving graduate school admission as their primary goal gained admission, as compared to 31 percent of all respondents. Fifty-five percent of those who selected "intelligent citizen participation in social work matters in the community" thought that they participated in civic affairs more than their acquaintances, as compared to 33 percent of the total alumni respondents. In light of the findings on vocational goals and objectives, we shall concern ourselves primarily with education for employment in this paper. Table I summarizes the variation among types of respondents with regard to educational goals.

Educational Objectives Must Be Compatible
with Utilization Patterns

As a qualifying statement concerning the objectives of undergraduate education, we would like to define social work employment broadly, isolate common roles, and indicate relevant knowledge and skills which may be used in a variety of helping professions. This approach seems advisable in light of program developments at the federal level and the growing professional recognition that segmentation of helping service education has yielded insufficient knowledge

TABLE I

PRIMARY GOALS OF UNDERGRADUATE SOCIAL WORK EDUCATION AS SELECTED BY GRADUATES, AGENCIES, AND INSTRUCTORS

Primary Goal	Respondents							
	Graduates		Agencies		Wis. & FSU Instructors		Other Instructors	
	No.	%	No.	%	No.	%	No.	%
Employment	289	64	78	75.0	24	69	63	88.8
Grad. School, Social Work	60	13	10	9.6	5	14	2	2.8
Community Participation	52	12	8	7.7	0	0	1	1.4
Same as any other Major	50	11	8	7.7	6	17	5	7.0
TOTALS	451	100	104	100.0	35	100	71	100.0

and skill to meet the public demand for effectiveness. For example, half of the FSU-BSW's who obtained jobs following graduation in the first half of 1971 found them in manpower, tutor-guidance, or social educator positions. Success rates for those preferring social work employment were: 1966, 100%; 1967, 86.7%; 1968, 81.2%; 1969, 80.5%; 1970, 70.7%; 1971, 65.7%. A confirmed scarcity of jobs for baccalaureate-level social work graduates indicates that the helping service market will continue to be broadly explored by those seeking work. Some schools might well have heeded the sage advice of Dean Ernest Witte:

> Keep the undergraduate program in social welfare generic. This would recognize the need and validity for developing an integrated learning experience for students with a potential career interest in all of the social services (sometimes called the 'helping services') including corrections (both adult and youth), school counselling, employment services, public assistance, social insurance, group services for young people (scouting, recreation, etc.), community development, child welfare, services for the aging, and health services.[2]

The need to evaluate graduate social work education in light of current trends is equally important. We need not labor this point to fellow educators who are trying to make adjustments to the professional incorporation of the undergraduate curriculum and to create a viable client-social system approach with reduced budgets. But, in summary, we conceive of the undergraduate social work major as a generalist with a central Broker-advocate function, with other levels of education supplying narrower and more specialized functions. Information and referral service would be performed by a systems specialist with a low-key advocacy responsibility. Appropriate knowledge must accompany professional values and skills in insuring adequate worker performance.

The Relevance of Social Science Content to Social Work

Primarily, social science concepts can provide a framework for the utilization of methodologies designed for making disciplined observations prerequisite to the construction and testing of hypothesis. Historically, statistical methods and case analysis have augmented hypothesis testing

and observation in the use of data to describe the function
of systems and to make at least crude predictions of the
impact of social change and social policies.   Furthermore,
theory can be related to individual and social needs in the
origination of developmental strategies to improve individual
and group welfare.   Granted that the social sciences are
far from conceptually perfect and sometimes inconsistent in
definition of terms, there is still no justification for not
utilizing pertinent knowledge when its validity has been
demonstrated.

Recent Professional Concern

A few years ago, Mary Burns of the University of
Michigan wrote:

> A review of the current state of social work knowl-
> edge discloses a devastating lack of agreement as
> to the definition of many of the concepts in use.
> Frames of reference are vague and general, and
> theories are either so comprehensive that they are
> difficult to render into practice principles or so
> limited at the practice principle level that they
> are seldom applicable.   Middle-level theory, from
> which practice principles can be derived, is large-
> ly missing.   Practice knowledge has been only in-
> adequately codified, and practice wisdom is largely
> unvalidated.   The net result is that, in any of the
> practice methods by which social work seeks to
> achieve its ultimate aims, professional social
> workers must function with a body of knowledge
> that at best is imprecise, at worst erroneous,
> and always is inadequate and difficult to communi-
> cate. [3]

Professor Burns advocated inputs from the social and behavioral sciences as one approach to the cleaning of our professional Augean Stables.   Others who expressed similar
criticism of the clinical or medical model were Eveline
Burns and Gilbert Geis. [4]

In further support of greater social science integration, Mereb Mossman succinctly stated:

> Since the field of social work is concerned funda-
> mentally with man interacting with society,

considerable content from the social sciences is
relevant. We have identified some concepts and
areas of content which we believe have particular
significance because they contribute knowledge of
the socio-cultural, political and economic context
of social welfare. [5]

The particular need for more knowledge of economics and
political science has also been advocated by Kendall, Piven
and others, but content integration has moved slowly. [6]

The Systems-Role-Knowledge Paradigm

There have been several attempts to define social
worker roles in terms of present needs of clients, the public, existing agencies, and the social work profession. [7]
Major contributors include Carol Meyer, [8] Eugene Koprowski,
Herbert Bisno, Teare and McPheeters, and Max Siporin. [9]
One of the best-known efforts, sponsored by the Southern
Regional Education Board, enumerated the roles of outreach,
social brokerage, advocacy, evaluation, data managing,
teaching, behavior changing, mobilizing, consulting, community planning, care giving, and administering. [10] It was
conceived that a generalist in a small agency might be expected to perform all roles or that in others, related
clusters could be included in worker job functions in harmony with agency programs; e.g., in a client-oriented
agency, the first eight roles might comprise the major functions of a social worker. The importance of social and behavioral science knowledge becomes evident when one ex-
amines the various kinds of obstacles to the attainment of
effective services. The worker must consider governmental
systems, especially service availability and transportation;
market system potential and payment sources related to the
economic system; the family system for its supportive possibilities; knowledge furnished through educational systems;
motivation as understood through the context of the behavioral sciences; and the legal structure, including structural
and functional knowledge of public welfare services with
existent gaps and other limitations.

Our responses from undergraduate social work alumni, agencies and instructors (N = 880) yielded the following
ranking of the functions of undergraduate-trained social
workers. Eleven items were ranked, then paired in SREB
roles, hence the 4.05-9.04 range of means.

TABLE II

RANKING OF IMPORTANCE OF RELATED CONTENT AREAS BY FIVE SOCIAL WORK FACULTY GROUPS

(most to least important)

| Disciplines | Aldridge-McGrath Study (N=860)[11] | | Pearman-McLean Study | | | | | | | |
	Rank	Percent	All = 152 Rank	Mean	Wisconsin = 20 Rank	Mean	FSU = 24 Rank	Mean	Others = 108 Rank	Mean
Sociology	1	(91)	1	(1.41)	1	(2.17)	1	(1.67)	1	(1.22)
History	2	(78)								
Economics	3	(77)	3	(3.70)	3	(3.50)	3	(3.58)	4	(3.76)
Political Science	4	(73)	2	(3.03)	2	(3.17)	2	(2.96)	2	(3.03)
Literature	5	(67)	7	(5.99)	7	(5.82)	7	(5.48)	7	(6.16)
Philosophy	6	(61)	6	(5.14)	5	(4.25)	5	(4.96)	6	(5.32)
Anthropology			4	(3.74)	4	(3.56)	4	(3.83)	3	(3.75)
Statistics & Res.			5	(4.90)	6	(5.22)	6	(5.38)	5	(4.74)

TABLE III

RANKINGS OF DISCIPLINES WHICH FACILITATE THE UNDERSTANDING OF SOCIAL SYSTEMS BY FIVE FACULTY GROUPS

Discipline	7 Referees		All = 152		Wisconsin = 20		FSU = 24		Others = 108	
	Rank	Mean	Rank	Mean	Rank	Mean	Rank	Mean	Rank	Mean
Sociology	1	(1.29)	1	(2.05)	1	(2.28)	1	(2.38)	1	(1.93)
Political Science	2	(2.86)	3	(3.15)	2	(3.22)	2	(2.88)	3	(3.20)
Anthropology	3	(3.43)	5	(4.76)	5	(4.22)	6	(4.87)	5	(5.03)
Economics	4	(3.86)	4	(4.07)	4	(4.11)	4	(3.67)	4	(4.16)
Philosophy	5	(4.71)	7	(6.13)	7	(5.25)	7	(6.09)	7	(6.26)
Social Work as an Institution	6	(5.17)	2	(2.69)	3	(3.61)	3	(3.25)	2	(2.37)
U.S. History	7	(5.86)	6	(5.07)	6	(4.76)	5	(4.88)	6	(5.17)

2. Likewise, social work instructors logically need much graduate training in the social sciences as well as in social work. Without this we cannot expect effective bridging of social science knowledge into viable problem-solving methods. Educational backgrounds do not suggest extensive knowledge of social sciences on the part of a large portion of graduate and undergraduate facilities. Onken[13] reported that 60 percent of graduate faculties had not taken course work above the MSW. Our current research on undergraduate social work instruction revealed 39 percent reporting the MSW only and 32 percent reporting a year or more of graduate study other than the MSW. Of 103 respondents outside the University of Wisconsin-Madison and Florida State University faculties, 41 percent reported the MSW only and 32 percent reported a year or more of graduate study in addition to the MSW. Related research conducted by Pearman and Jahns in 1970 revealed that 46 percent of undergraduate social work instructors and 66 percent of those primarily teaching methods had less than one year of graduate study beyond the MSW.

Respondents ranked sociology (1), political science (2), and economics (3) as to content area importance (see Table II), but 29 percent thought that undergraduate programs should be best strengthened by hiring MSW's with practice experience, 24 percent indicated no preference as to specific education, and only 24 percent indicated preference for an MSW with at least a year in sociology, political science and/or economics. Only five percent indicated a preference for MSW's with a year or more of graduate study in psychology and/or anthropology. The question arises as to whether undergraduate instructors thought a strong systems orientation to be important, and if so, did they consider graduate social science study essential for teachers who are trying to accomplish this purpose? Yet 51 percent of the instructor respondents thought that many content areas, such as anthropology, psychology and economics, should be required of undergraduate social work majors. Again, how can instructors bridge social science without relevant knowledge?

3. Efforts on the part of teachers to integrate social science theory and social work practice must be rewarded rather than censored. Rather complex, and sometimes conceptually difficult, social science theory and relevant empirical data do not appeal strongly to many students or faculties. Also, faculty members with a strong policy or

community organization orientation may more frequently be
censured than pitied. In the day of the student as the master of curriculum planning, with student evaluation of teachers important to salary increases and promotion, and budget
allotments in terms of class enrollments, rewards may not
be forthcoming for faculty who are academically ambitious
in helping students to incorporate social science knowledge.
There may be a symbiotic student-faculty gain in deception
as to teaching inputs and learning outputs. Where such
counter-productive conditions do exist, students, faculty and
administration must recast objectives in harmony with major
goals, plan constructive change and install positive evaluative
methods related to predetermined criteria. We have for
much too long expected evaluation on demand-related inputs
instead of longer term outputs in relation to objective criteria.

An Approach to Greater Social Science
Utilization in Social Work

        Suggestions for incorporation of social science knowl-
edge into social work, with some sophisticated models, have
been presented by social work educators. But the soil must
be prepared and cultivated before the crop can be harvested.
Otherwise, contributions such as Romanyshyn's text, Social
Welfare, are limited in value in raising the conceptual level
of social science inputs utilized by social workers.

        1. Our first recommendation is a comprehensive
program of educating social work instructors at all levels,
including field instructors who have the responsibility for
the practical application to social work concepts. We share
the view of Harold Enarson, Vice President of the University of New Mexico, who made the following recommendation:

                ... it's time continuing education was built into
                the academic enterprise as a central article of
                faith. The rich and varied diet of short courses,
                institute, and evening classes listed in our cata-
                logs are a tribute to zeal, but they do not repre-
                sent a commitment to the proposition that life-long
                learning has become a necessity for all of us in
                this quick-changing society. It is not simply engi-
                neers and doctors who need retreading. Political
                scientists, educators, social workers, and

community leaders also need the discipline of formal instruction. The tooling and retooling of the
mind is the primary task of colleges and universities. The social systems that make up a community are more complex than our theories of our
professional faiths are prepared to admit. We had
better recognize the 'community' for the compli-
cated enterprise that it is, and be prepared to
take time to study it carefully if we are to be effective. 14

The importance of social systems and social science
knowledge is further recognized in governmental program
drifts and by professional accrediting agencies, as previously
noted in reference to the transmittal letter from Lillian
Ripple, Acting Director, Council on Social Work Education.

2. Undergraduate majors, who now have an enlarged
professional role, must be held academically responsible in
all facets of their education, especially in the social sciences, rather than relying on methods courses alone to develop effectiveness. We suggest a broad exposure to the
social and behavioral sciences through a year's work in at
least three disciplines, with at least one social science
minor required. Graduate requirements should be increased
accordingly and, if students are admitted without the level
of social science background indicated above, then the graduate student should be required to make up the deficiency
through taking graduate or undergraduate credit courses for
credit.

3. Administrators must consider the difficulties
faced in transferring social science knowledge to social
work practice in passing out rewards. Operant psychology
must be applied positively. Universities should offer more
remunerative incentive to take study leaves or concurrent
course work.

4. With the above adjustments, as suggested by
Bloom, 15 an information retrieval team comprised of generalists and specialists, operating within a computerized
support system, could then consider social and behavioral
science knowledge for relevancy in social work practice and
help teachers develop middle-level theory and strategies
based on significant fact and concepts. Each faculty member should have sufficient education to accomplish much on
his own, but a retrieval team could help, especially if the

faculties and retrieval teams were prepared to play in the
same or similar ballgames.

Notes

1. The stark reality of the relationship between the future
    of social work education and public values, as re-
    flected in developing programs, is recognized in a
    transmittal letter, dated February 2, 1972, on pro-
    gramming and funding opportunities for schools of
    social work. Lillian Ripple, Acting Director of the
    Council on Social Work Education states, "Our con-
    tinuing efforts to identify programming and funding
    opportunities for schools of social work convinces
    us more than ever that actual availability of funds
    will depend to a large degree upon the clarity of
    the mission of the school and/or the scope of its
    present programs or future plans and emphases.
    More importantly, support will be related to the
    ability of schools of social work to develop rela-
    tionships and establish credibility with state agencies
    that are related to specific national priorities and
    concerns. "

2. Arnulf M. Pins, editor, Continuities In Undergraduate
    Education. New York: Council on Social Work
    Education, 1969. See 'Implications and Next Steps
    for Undergraduate Education" by Ernest F. Witte,
    p. 65.

3. Mary E. Burns, "Paths to Knowledge: Some Prospects
    and Problems, " Journal Of Education For Social
    Work, v. 1, Spring 1965, pp. 13-14.

4. Eveline Burns, "Tomorrow's Social Needs and Social
    Work Education, " Journal Of Education For Social
    Work, v. 2, Spring 1966, pp. 10-21; Gilbert Geis,
    "Liberal Education for Social Welfare; Educational
    Choices and their Consequences, " Journal Of Educa-
    tion For Social Work, v. 1, Spring 1965, pp. 26-
    32.

5. Mereb E. Mossman, "Current Undergraduate Social
    Service Education: Developing Structures, " Regional
    Institute on Undergraduate Social Service Education,
    Salt Lake City. Boulder: Western Interstate

Commission for Higher Education, May, 1965, p. 14.

6. Katherine Kendall in "Undergraduate Preparation for Social Services," Continuities In Undergraduate Social Welfare Education, op. cit., pp. 82-83; and Frances Fox Piven, "Political Science Content and the Social Work Curriculum," Social Work Education Reporter, v. 15, June 1967, pp. 26-27.

7. See J. R. Pearman and Winnifred Thomet, "Professional Implications for Social Work in a Cybernetic State," Science Studies, v. 2, April 1972, for a discussion of the impact of social change on the social work process.

8. Social Work Practice. New York: The Free Press, 1970.

9. See J. R. Pearman and Irwin R. Jahns, "The Diffusion of an Innovative Methods Model into Course Content," accepted for publication by the Social Work Education Reporter, (April-May, 1973), and available in mimeographed form from the National Conference on Social Welfare.

10. Robert J. Teare and Harold L. McPheeters, Manpower Utilization In Social Welfare. Atlanta: Southern Regional Education Board, 1970.

11. Gordon J. Aldridge and Earl J. McGrath, Liberal Education and Social Work. New York: Teachers College Press, Columbia University, 1965, p. 52.

12. G. J. Aldridge and E. J. McGrath, op. cit., p. 60.

13. Richard Onken, A Survey of Faculty in Graduate Schools of Social Work. New York: Council on Social Work Education, 1968, pp. 25-56.

14. Harold L. Enarson, "Social Services in the West: What Practice Needs," in Regional Institute on Undergraduate Social Service Education, edited by Roma K. McNickle. Boulder, 1965, p. 10.

15. Martin Bloom, "The Selection of Knowledge from Other Disciplines and its Integration into Social Work

Curricula, Journal Of Social Work Education, v. 5,
Spring 1969, pp. 15-29.

4. SOME COMMON CONCEPTS OF SOCIAL SCIENCE
   AND SOCIAL WELFARE*

Behavioral scientists, social scientists, and social workers once became lost in the trivia of the household, the two-or-more group, the axons, the dendrites and the Oedipus Complex. We are now seeking broad concepts which may some day negate the necessity of declaring an academic frame of reference before starting discussion. There are some terms and generalizations which have similar meaning in the social sciences and in such professional arts as teaching and social work. The macro-model is gaining increasing recognition and support as evidenced by the comprehensive Economic Opportunity Programs and such planning devices as systems analysis. Even the economist no longer stands outside the professional sociometric circle as a purely insensitive, brutal and stilted mechanistic monster.

Gordon Hamilton's persistent plea to put the "social" back into social work and more graphic comments up to and including Richard Titmuss' definition of traditional American social work as "the art of teaching people how to live in Hell," are being received positively rather than with indifference and skepticism. Barriers between theoretical and applied social science still exist, but they are starting to dissolve.

Increased reliance on the social sciences has been encouraged by dissatisfaction with current public welfare programs, the failures of professional caseworkers to provide adequately for persons in poverty sufficient inner strength to cope with massive external obstacles, poverty data and poverty program failures, to mention only a few determining forces. We have not abandoned individual

*Reprinted from Florida A and M University Research Bulletin 19 (June, 1970), pp. 41-47, with the permission of Charles U. Smith, Editor. The original title has been changed.

restoration as a legitimate goal, but we are thinking more
strenuously of prevention through more effective services
less hampered by heavy manpower investments in eligibility
determination.   Declarative financial statements, instead of
lengthy investigations, and the negative income tax are cases
in point.   But our efforts need to be supported by some accepted central concepts which are mutually understood and
generally accepted by social scientists and social workers.
This groundwork is essential to communication to the general public, so encouraging their acceptance of more effective welfare programs in relation to client needs.

Essential Social Science Concepts

This paper offers two major contentions relative to
academic effectiveness in the dissemination of social science
concepts which will stimulate improvement in social welfare
policies.

1.   There are some common concepts which cut
     across the confusing semantics of the social sci-
     ences and these concepts can be understood and
     applied by social workers and the general public.

2.   We have equally important concepts which influ-
     ence general welfare which may be harder to
     communicate but it is important for social work-
     ers and social policy shapers to gain and use
     these concepts.

Common Basic Concepts

1.   A central concept which is very much in evidence
in the social sciences and social work is development.
Elizabeth Wickenden points to the world-wide goals of abun-
dance and mutuality as being of interdisciplinary significance. [1]   Economics, which has received limited emphasis
in graduate social welfare education, may be used as an
example for potential integration.   The central focus of
economics is to get the greatest possible product out of
limited factors of production.   Just as social welfare attempts maximization in individual, group, and community
functioning, economic laws partially guide allocation, production, and consumption which, by the strength or weakness
of decision making, can strengthen or weaken satisfaction.

From the time of Adam Smith, mutuality of interest, at least in production, has been stressed by economists. Specialization in production and interdependency in exchange and distribution obviously necessitate a mutual interest in continuing activity on a level which best serves to meet individual needs. We have become increasingly aware of the role of social and economic planning in our endeavor to increase satisfaction of individuals. We now know that planning and development exist in a variety of political and economic systems throughout the world with the possibility that any given system might be better suited to meeting existing economic needs of individuals in one part of the world than in some other area. But expansion of production is not the only function of planning. Improvement of human and physical resources, foreign aid, foreign trade, domestic and foreign investment, monetary and fiscal policies of government. In fact, virtually all of the areas of economics have some bearing on planning and growth; e.g., we lower interest rates to encourage low cost housing loans, and we create trouble in the balance of payments and cause unwanted gold outflow. Development implies social change leading to a better ordering of relationships among people, their physical environment, and their social organizations which will provide a more satisfying life for all concerned. It has a common application in social science and social welfare and we need to gain a broad view of policy impact directed toward development, not only from the viewpoint of a given client, but also from the broad interdisciplinary, macro-viewpoint.

Social welfare, i.e., "those laws, programs, benefits and services which assure or strengthen provisions for meeting social needs recognized as basic to the well-being of the population and better functioning of the social order,"[2] is not a unique concept of social work experts. Economics has a similar purpose. Welfare economics, using the crude measure of the popular consumption criterion,[3] is significant to the maximizing of satisfaction of all individuals. Allocation of goods and services in the direction of need and desire is important whether accomplished in the free or partially free market or by the government. Social welfare programs are potentially important in individual and social development through getting goods to people which they most want and need.

Public welfare programs cannot be tested in the conventional market place, but some principles of economics can be used to judge the effectiveness of programs. As allocation is made in favor of one program over another, one needs always to keep in mind the concept of opportunity cost, i. e. , that the cost of an outlay is the cost of an alternative on which an allocation might have been made. Continuous evaluation and research are essential to sound judgment in allocation to reach the goal of maximization of satisfaction. We are, therefore, seeking to perfect input-output research methods which will help make wise choices and establish the degree of accountability being achieved by existing programs.

2. Social change is a phenomenon known to all social sciences and to social work. Material and non-material changes occur frequently. As a change is constantly occurring, so are favorable and unfavorable consequences constantly developing. Change is being increasingly planned and less crescive or evolutionary. Virtually no aspect of human life is free from the expectation of the normality of change. Social change is related to cultural growth which is an accumulation of material and non-material traits. If associated with fixed value judgments, change may connote progress or decay, decadence, and degeneration. If a dynamic or mechanistic viewpoint is taken, social changes may be observed in terms of such social processes as adjustment, accommodation, and assimilation.

Although sociologists have shown leadership in developing the literature on social change and such related concepts as evolution and progress, change has meaning for economists and social workers. Change from rural to urban living affects markets and, consequently, the allocation of productive factors. Automation not only affects plant management, but also manpower utilization and welfare maximization. The uprooting that comes with horizontal and vertical mobility, from civilian to military, from nuclear family to independence, from country to city, may lead to a sense of insecurity. Old patterns of behavior may not fit new situations, and the attempt to use such socially latent patterns may lead to a heightening of frustration and personal and social disorganization. A better understanding of the concept of social change and its related components might have helped us avert some of the recent disastrous riots in our central cities.

Essential Concepts Requiring More Effective Dissemination

1. A concept of common academic usage is that of functionalism which focuses upon the unity and directness of a total system rather than upon mechanistic relationships between parts of a system. The Gestalt viewpoint has influenced social workers to view any part of a problem as a functional part of a whole, but this understanding must be community-related as well as client-related. The assumption of validity of existing norms and the acceptance of reality as a fixed entity around which adjustments in individual behavior are to be made, suggest functionalist thinking. In economics, classical and neo-classical economists took a functional view when they assumed that natural individual differences would effect harmony in the economic realm. Policy makers who hold this view will either want to change the whole system or do nothing for fear that any change will produce major disorganization.

2. The functional concept is challenged by the mechanistic view which holds that the functioning of a specific part can influence the whole; thus, constraints of an internal nature, such as monopoly, or of an external nature, such as government aid and control, are applied selectively to influence the functioning of the economy. Caseworkers are mechanistic (or dynamic) when they seek to influence ego as a means of influencing social functioning. Other behavioral sciences, e. g., political science, anthropology, and psychology, also question functionalism as the most logical frame of reference and resort to a behavioristic approach. However, both viewpoints are found in present day behavioral science literature. 4 Advocates of social welfare policy change, who are mechanistic, will make selective changes in hopes of improving the total social system.

3. A central concept which has application in both the functional and mechanistic approaches is that of equilibrium which implies a balance of opposing forces in a state of affairs in which things are at rest. These things may be supply and demand, savings and investment, a balance between or among human needs and institutional function, or id, ego, and superego. Functional theories describe some relations within a system as self-regulating in the direction of equilibrium. The ego has this function in social work, as does the market price and saving in economics. The ego mediates among id, superego, and the reality factor. Market price corrects disequilibrium between supply and

demand. The ex post adjustment of investment to saving
through changes in the National Product corrects imbalance
on the macro-economics scene. Adjustment may be a more
common term in social work, but equilibrium would also be
a useful word for the concept.

4. It is my impression that a much larger list of
common concepts for social science and social work should
be developed. In the interest of time and space I will venture past one more--that of marginality. In sociology,
marginal man is one who lives between two cultures with a
sense of anomie, or in more current language, powerless-
ness. In economics, the marginal laborer is one who will
just return his cost in production. In social work, a marginal person is one whose ego is barely able to sustain an
acceptable level of social functioning. We have not achieved
sufficient integration of social science knowledge into social
welfare policy determination and social work practice. We
need to face the barriers which stand in the way.

Theory Barriers

One great problem among the social sciences and between the social sciences and social work is that of communication. Various authorities within a specific discipline
have trouble in speaking to each other. For example, social workers experience difficulty in trying to integrate
economic laws and principles into social welfare policy
courses because it is hard to reconcile the physical science
model of economics with the lower level theory conceptualization of social work. Consequently to some social workers, economists become cruel inhuman sadists who think
only in terms of production schedules. To some economists,
social workers appear as naive victims of passion and compassion with little regard for rationality. To some social
workers, sociologists are highly paid census enumerators
producing useless statistics; to some sociologists, social
workers are far-out chamber pot determinists.

Perception-of-System Barriers

Again turning to economics for an example, competition is the sine qua non of free enterprise. Controls, public or private, are inconsistent with the ideal free enterprise economy. Some economic illiterates think that they

are upholding a free enterprise system when they attack certain governmental services or controls such as social security, Great Society Programs, or housing programs. No mention may be given of the fact that approximately one-half of the federal government bureaus are designed to furnish a welfare service to business. 5 Actually, the United States has a system of limited capitalism involving free enterprise, monopoly control, government control and government ownership.

An important consideration relative to the role of government is that of establishing theoretically and actually the effectiveness of competition. Competition may be of service to humanity. Differences as to competition's actual effectiveness vary with (1) differences in interpretation as to what motivates the individual, (2) the degree to which pure competition is possible, (3) whether government or business control is best where competition is thought to be undesirable, and (4) whether government interference with a specific process, e. g. , distribution, actually aids that process and, if so, whether the interference hinders other processes. But one fact cannot be denied. Our basic capitalistic system makes no provision for those who are not producers and government must intervene with welfare or comprehensive minimum income plans such as the negative income tax to insure life and decent living to millions of nonproducers.

Lack of Clarity of the Total Welfare Picture

As we have indicated, even if we reduce the functioning of the market as a point of emphasis, there is ample relevant content in economics without this significant knowledge area. If we cannot extricate welfare considerations from the constraints of market functioning, poor law philosophy still reigns. And the voice of the client-consumer is to be heard even though he will not be speaking through dollar votes in the market.

Perhaps a new perspective on a part of welfare policy, that part which pertains to governmental programs, can be gained through the following of the direction pointed by Richard Titmuss. 6 He suggests that we consider social welfare from a much broader viewpoint than mere description of income maintenance and public health programs. Taking, for an example, one welfare consideration, the

redistribution effect of welfare policies, Titmuss shows how
the non-discrimination principle and favoritism in the direction of the more affluent, inherent in certain welfare programs, e. g , education and housing, may actually negate
some of the redistributive effects of other programs so far
as lower income groups are concerned. In addition, we
have to judge the impact on fiscal welfare and occupational
welfare of such fringe compensations as survivors' benefits,
severance pay, travel allowances, tax exemptions, meal
vouchers, residential accommodations, cars, season tickets,
and many other benefits of redistributive impact which need
attention to get the total picture. Sound welfare, fiscal welfare, and occupational welfare programs all have a redistributive effect and the student interested in poverty and distribution of income needs to understand the significance of
all welfare programs. We must place the broad picture of
a welfare-oriented society and economic welfare in the same
perspective. The development of comprehensive statistics
on social indicators may assist our perspective.

In summary, we need to replace emotional, unrea-
soned judgment with rational analysis. Reasoned choice involves (1) definition of the problem facing us, (2) identifying
goals and priorities, (3) considering alternatives in the application of limited resources, and (4) analyzing consequences
of alternatives before and after each choice is made. Cost-
benefit analysis may provide the necessary tools. The above
reasoned-choice requirements can be used equally well in a
discussion of economic planning, administrative evaluation,
or in a discussion of effective ego-functioning.

                                Notes

1.   Elizabeth Wickenden, Social Welfare in a Changing
         World.   Washington, D. C. : U. S. Department of
         Health, Education and Welfare, 1965, pp. 1-2.

2.   Ibid. , p. vii.

3.   John K. Galbraith, Economic Development.   Cambridge:
         Harvard University Press, 1967, p. 11.

4.   Don Martindale, editor, Functionalism in the Social Sci-
         ences.   Philadelphia: American Academy of Political
         and Social Sciences, 1965, p. 65-75.

5.   "The Spreading of State Welfare," Fortune 45 (February, 1952), 102-3.

6.   Richard M. Titmuss, "The Role of Redistribution in Social Policy," Social Security Bulletin 28 (June 1965), 14-20.

Bibliography

Burns, Eveline, "Tomorrow's Social Needs and Social Work Education," Journal of Education for Social Work, v. 2, no. 1, Spring, 1966, pp. 10-20.

Galbraith, John K., Economic Development.   Cambridge: Harvard University Press, 1967.

Irving, Howard H., "A Social Science Approach to a Problem in Field Instruction: The Analysis of a Three-part Role Set," Journal of Education for Social Work, v. 5, no. 1, Spring, 1969, pp. 49-56.

Maas, Henry S., "Collaboration Between Social Work and the Social Sciences," Social Work Journal, v. 31, no. 3, July, 1950, pp. 104-110.

Martindale, Don, editor, Functionalism in the Social Sciences, a monograph.   Philadelphia: The American Academy of Political and Social Sciences, February, 1965.

National Academy of Sciences, The Behavioral and Social Sciences: Outlook and Needs.   Washington, D.C., 1969.

Pollak, Otto, "Contributions of Sociological and Psychological Theory to Casework Practice, Journal of Education for Social Work, v. 4, no. 1, Spring, 1968, pp. 49-54.

Silverman, Irving, Richard Bretman, Fred Suffet and Dale Ordes, "Reaching for Accountability in Community Practice," Public Health Reports, v. 85, no. 3, March, 1970, pp. 251-266.

Titmuss, Richard M., "The Role of Redistribution in Social Policy," Social Security Bulletin, v. 28, no. 6, June, 1965, pp. 14-20.

Wickenden, Elizabeth, Social Welfare in a Changing World.

Washington, D. C. :   United States Department of Health,
Education and Welfare, 1965.

PART II

THE IMPACT OF SOCIAL CHANGE ON
SOCIAL SYSTEMS AND PROFESSIONAL ROLES

Part II provides theoretical and empirical information concerning relationships between and among social change, values and human needs, social systems, and professional roles. The implications of an increased use of cybernetics, and science of communication and control of systems, especially as regards welfare service delivery, are far-reaching. New technologies induce changes in agency structure and function, so altering manpower needs in much the same way that job functions changed in the transition from the horse-drawn buggy to the automobile as the major means of individualized transportation. The magic of professional status tends to evaporate if the accountability of professional practice is not established through proven evaluative techniques. Governmental funding depends largely on how well helping service education can meet the effectiveness expectations of new programs and revamped health, education, and welfare systems. Efficiency in proper utilization of planned inputs can be monitored by computerized control devices using feedback sub-systems.

The following chapters document some current role demands, and possible positive and negative professional reactions to change are analyzed in terms of established sociological concepts. A means of achieving greater compatibility of social work with social systems expectations is suggested in the developmental-role-task model in which professional roles are redefined in harmony with changing needs. A case is made for greater utilization of relevant

theory from several social sciences as the functional value
of social science input into a systems-oriented methodology
is illustrated.

Variations in the attitudes of professional social work
educators toward change and the growth of competition for
emerging roles in related helping professions are described.
Change resistance by social work and other helping service
educators and practitioners is documented through research
on the diffusion of the developmental-role-task model into
course content, and some of the variables influencing innovation are explored. Rapid change calls for a truly dynamic
approach to helping rather than a commitment to the status
quo and a faith in a professional power to change individual
life styles through concentration on a counseling relationship
controlled by a set of values which may be alien to the cli-
ent-target.

5. PROFESSIONAL IMPLICATIONS FOR SOCIAL WORK
   IN A CYBERNETIC STATE*

      Discussions of the relationship between technological
change and the structure and functions of social organizations
are not new. Ogburn,[1] and many later sociologists, developed the "cultural lag" theory of change and social disorganization. Later theoretical improvements, such as that
of Arnold Rose,[2] have pointed to the decline of human need
fulfillment within social systems, and a consequent reduction
in the predictability of the behavior of individuals and groups
--with the resulting formation of conflicting sub-cultures and
anomic retreat into individual pathologies. Karl Marx, Ralf
Dahrendorf, Lewis Coser, and Amitai Etzioni have further
elaborated the role of conflict in social change.[3]

      Donald A. Schon has succinctly stated this relation-
ship between technological change and social organization:

> Social and technological systems interlock. An
> apparently innocuous change in technology may
> emerge as a serious threat to an organization be-
> cause it would force it to transform its theory and
> structure. Technological, theoretical and social
> systems exist as aspects of one another; change
> in one provokes change in the others. And change
> in organizations has its impact on the person, be-
> cause beliefs, values and the sense of self have
> their being in social systems.[4]

It follows that system changes will produce a need for new
or altered roles for professionals, which they may or may
not actively participate in shaping.

_____

*Published with the consent of the co-author, Winnifred M.
Thomet, Graduate School of Social Work, Rutgers University,
and the original publisher, MacMillan Journals, Ltd., in
Science Studies, v. 2 (1972), pp. 181-190.

Cultural growth and improved levels of living are products of innovation and diffusion. The increased speed of diffusion yields more rapid change, and is accompanied by confusion and conflict. Time-honored theory is challenged. For example, equilibrium, or functional, theorists see change as a transitory disruption between levels of stability; they assume that society has built-in controls which limit the destabilizing impact of changing technology. But contrary evidence is now to be found in the degraded countryside, in decayed cities and in worldwide disorder. We have been forced to view change as continuous and dynamic, and our main concern seems to be over the apparent incapacity of major social systems adequately to meet needs, and to restore a feeling of stability. We are searching for new tools to reduce the negative aspects of constructive change, and for a means of avoiding changes which do not serve to enhance the general welfare. Conflict may draw attention to system failures, but it does not ensure corrective institutional change. In a dynamic society, we need analytical tools which will better describe problems, and help to devise constructive changes in systems. Donald Schön, for instance, seeks the development of a learning system within agency structures which will bring about continuous adjustments in harmony with changing values and needs. [5]

The Cybernetic Technology

The most dramatic and disruptive, yet potentially corrective, technological change of the current age is cybernation. The use of computers goes beyond the previous automation of sensory and motor tasks into the areas of routine and complex logical deductions and decision making; in so doing it partially replaces a function previously conceived of as "essentially human." The computer out-performs people in calculative precision, speed, detection and correction of errors, harmony with programmed instructions, and the retention and recall of original input and newly-generated data. Developments in the weighing of strategies based on accumulated data are extending this "think" capacity of computers, and increasing their advantages. Costs can be cut, the obligation of management towards human relations may be reduced, the rationality of decision-making improved, diverse branches and elements coordinated, and social controls made increasingly effective. But computer application in the production of goods and services is not an unmixed blessing. Donald N. Michael's conclusions on the probable impact of cybernation, although written a decade ago, are showing increased relevance:

> ... But as cybernation advances, new and profound
> problems will arise for our society and its values.
> Cybernation presages changes in the social system
> so vast and so different from those with which we
> have traditionally wrestled that it will challenge to
> their roots our current perceptions about the via-
> bility of our way of life. If our democratic sys-
> tem has a chance to survive at all, we shall need
> far more understanding of the consequences of
> cybernation. Even the job of simply preserving a
> going society will take a level of planning far ex-
> ceeding any of our previous experiences with cen-
> tralized control. [6]

Cybernetics (and other technological change) has brought a
need for adjustment in both broad and limited social systems. We need planned change, but we cannot avoid disruption and disorganization. Innovation is not a perfectly
rational, step-by-step process. Trial and error, pragmatic
program changes, and exploitation of chance developments,
are components of the process of invention. Uncertainty
cannot be eliminated, but it can be reduced through the use
of computers. [7]

The Evolution of the Cybernetic State

In democratic, industrialized societies, there has
been a progression from initial concern about human liberties to a focus on control, and on the productive efficiency
of government in a complex social system. We are experiencing the built-in conflict inherent in the Weber model of
bureaucracy, between discipline and the increase of efficiency
by constructive feedback. [8] Allen Schick[9] has defined four
evolutionary states, each of which, of course, retains some
of the characteristics of earlier stages:

1. The political state sought to define individual liberty, and to construct constraints on the power of the state.
Concepts of representative government, check-and-balance
systems, and specific guarantees of rights of the individual
were developed.

2. The administrative state sought to maintain a

balance of power vis-à-vis business and industry which would
preserve workable competition, and counter the Marxist suggestion of absolute economic determinism. Legislative,
executive, and judicial decisions sought a balance, conceptu-
alized by Galbraith[10] as a countervailing power system.
Efforts were made towards developing expertise, civil service career ladders and specialization, and objectivity in
public administration.

3. The bureaucratic state, which has developed rapidly during the past four decades, has moved increasingly
towards governmental operation of business, and the provision of welfare services and income benefits. Consequently, lobbying efforts have multiplied as groups sought to de-
fend against, or gain from, the growth of governmental involvement in production and distribution. Advantages have
usually rested with the affluent (with possible exceptions in
Great Britain and the Scandinavian countries). But in the
United States, the comment is being increasingly heard that
welfare represents a system of "socialism for the rich and
free enterprise for the poor." During the hey-day of the
bureaucratic model, much advice was sought from professionals. Social workers had an appreciable influence on
policies and this led to an increased emphasis on services
as compared to income maintenance, a reduction in the size
of caseloads, and humane value implications in legislation.
For example, the 1962 amendments to the Social Security
Acts greatly increased federal matching of service costs, as
compared to financial benefits, in state public assistance
programs. But advice was frequently a matter of professional opinion, rather than the product of analytical research
which had proved the effectiveness of the recommended service methods.

4. We are just entering what may be termed the
cybernetic state. Legislators, the courts, and government
administrators are now insisting on specific goals, in which
the degree of goal fulfillment is amenable to more discrete
measurement. In the public arena, there is a declining interest in such general purposes as effecting self-fulfillment,
rendering service, enhancing growth, and fostering development. Emerging legislative and administrative policies suggest that these admirable general goals must be broken down
into specific and measurable objectives to meet new system
expectations. Values are still fundamental, but agency purposes must become definable in specific terms. The human
role then becomes one of monitoring the input, process and

output, and using the data to evaluate the possible advantages of alternative strategies. Sidney Fine has described the new focus:

> Why is a master purpose so important to the initi-
> ation of a systems approach? The answer is
> multi-faceted. To begin with, the determination
> of a purpose is a decision about values. Purposes
> emerge from many values and needs, which are
> more or less in competition with one another. A
> decision to go one way rather than another is an
> assertion about priorities which provides a frame-
> work for later selecting among options to get the
> job done. Second, the purpose is indicative of the
> scope of the conception, including both the subsys-
> tems that will make it up and the larger system
> of which it is a part. Third, purpose generates
> the criteria according to which the progress of
> the system towards its goal will be continuously
> evaluated. Specification of the organizational pur-
> pose makes it possible to penetrate to what an
> organization actually does, rather than to accept
> on the verbal description level what it says it
> does. 11

Demands for increased effectiveness in American public welfare administration in the cybernetic state have raised the
issue of "accountability," and led to much confusion. For
the notion of accountability has at least two aspects: that
money be spent for the purposes for which it was appropriated, under defined rules of eligibility; and that social services bring about those individual and group changes in behavior which Congress, and the public, expects. Previously, decisions on eligibility were made, and social casework
services were provided, by the same agency--and, frequently, by the same worker. But following the 1967 Social Security amendments there has been a separation of functions:
on the one hand, eligibility determination (so that the distribution of funds can be measured and controlled under program planning and budget analysis); and, on the other, social services (in which improved measures of effectiveness
are continually being sought). No longer will the client be
expected to accept manipulation of his behavior as the price
he pays for receiving financial aid. Existing inadequacies
have led to frequent trial-and-error modifications. There
is some suggestion of change for the sake of change. Effective external or periphery leadership is a pressing need

of systems reform.

Regrettably, the preparation of social workers for a more effective role in systems change (including the addition of an effective learning component which will make agencies more responsive to client and community needs), may have been hampered by the limited academic preparation of graduate social work faculties. A report of the Council on Social Work Education on 475 doctorates employed in graduate schools of social work, lists the following numbers of doctorates by disciplines: sociology, family and social science, 71; psychology, social relations and group dynamics, 41; economics, 9; government, political science and public administration, 9. [12]

Program developers appear to be turning to disciplines outside social work for answers that were previously sought from social workers. State personnel recruitment announcements are including additional educational alternatives. For example, Illinois includes masters degrees in education and psychology with social work in recruiting requirements for child welfare program administrators, and New York includes the masters in public administration with social work in qualifications for public welfare administrators. Personnel interests of those who administer new approaches to solving major social welfare problems are further reflected in a recent pilot study conducted by the Bureau of Labor Statistics. [13] In the five cities studied there were several positions which might well be considered the province of social work, but only in one instance was social work mentioned as an alternative educational requirement. This was in the case of neighborhood development counselors, where social work was given equal billing with social science and vocational counseling. Work in community action, manpower development, planning, and community relations administration, and positions at lower levels, such as community relations workers, recreation specialists, social planning analysts, urban planners and urban renewal workers, did not include social work as an alternative educational specialization. Considering all listings, the number of times the following educational specializations appeared were: social science, 11; government and public administration, 7; economics, 5; sociology, 2; psychology, 1; and social work, 1. The preliminary reports of the US Health, Education and Welfare task force on the Family Assistance Plan also emphasize competence in public administration, interagency and intergovernmental relationships, policy and

planning, public relations and claims taking.[14] A very
serious question, related to such personnel trends, is
whether there will be sufficient sensitivity and knowledge in
these administrative teams to ensure early and efficient
referral to social work service agencies.   If not, preventive
potentialities may be greatly reduced.   The need for improved awareness of social systems, and of the social sciences generally, has not gone unnoticed among social work
educators, but there is doubt as to whether the impact of
change on the social work profession is adequately recognized.

Implications for Social Work

Vested interests in health and welfare organizations
are not entirely receptive to innovations which threaten the
prestige of administrators, and of recognized professionals.
Consequently, response to change may take the forms of
(1) direct opposition; (2) compartmentalization (i. e. , letting
the technician do his thing, but not permitting the new technology to disrupt existing patterns); (3) limiting the impact
of the innovation by restricted use within the existing system; (4) negative use in the acquisition and use of power,
if the innovation can be used to reduce the functions of
middle management and skilled professionals;[15] and (5) constructive application of the innovation to improve quality and
quantity productivity, reduce costs, and discover new roles
which professional and sub-professional personnel may fill.

Social workers might well devote more effort to determining how new goals can be related to researched needs,
and how new roles can be developed to assure the effectiveness of public welfare programs, and the successful solution
of individual and social problems.   In the current crises,
professional apprehension is great.   In addition to making a
more effective contribution to the shaping of new or altered
systems, social work has the challenge of revising theory
and technological methods to meet new values and needs.

The Developmental Role-Task Approach

It is obvious that the general functions of study, diagnosis and treatment, and methods or roles such as community organization, group work and casework, do not supply
concrete definitions which satisfy the emerging emphasis on

"supervisory monitoring. " The need has arisen for more
specific definitions of roles and tasks, and some progress
is being made in this direction. [16] Teare and McPheeters[17]
have used theoretical and observational studies to propose
a regrouping of social work activity in terms of (1) target
(client, family, or community); (2) objectives (behavior
change, environmental control or resource mobilization);
(3) routine tasks (eligibility determination or book-keeping);
(4) worker characteristics (education and experience as related to the roles of social work aide, therapist, or researcher); and (5) logistics (activity centered in office, neighborhood or city). They have further defined functional roles
as (1) outreach (involving the detection of people with problems, leading them to help, and providing follow up); (2)
social broker (providing information and referral, or other
bridging functions between systems and clients); (3) advocate
(pleading or fighting for agency services, or for a change
in the laws); (4) evaluator (involving gathering information,
assessing problems, weighing alternatives, and selecting
priorities); (5) teacher (providing conceptual and substantive
knowledge to increase the effectiveness of clients and staff);
(6) behavior changer (supplying coaching, counseling or
therapy); (7) mobilizer (developing new resources and programs); (8) consultant (upgrading skills of personnel); (9)
community planner (assisting in planning the structure and
function of systems so as to help meet clients' needs); (10)
care giver (providing direct supportive services to clients);
(11) data manager (including data gathering, tabulating,
analysis and synthesis); and (12) administration (involving
such activities as implementation of programs, personnel
relationships, fiscal control and supervision). The mush-
room growth of information and referral services in urban
areas of Great Britain, Canada and the United States is
evidence of the need for effective action in the areas of
broker, outreach, teacher and mobilizer.

The Transaction Process

        Herbert Bisno[18] has sought to clarify social work
roles through a focus on specific transactions. He distin-
guishes macro- and micro-system transactions: his macro-
systems include organizational and associational groups, in-
ter-group and community and other larger collectivities;
micro-system transactions involve one-to-one contacts and
other small groups. He views social work methods in terms
of specialized techniques and skills which are applied within

the client-worker relationship, and other similar transactional systems. His classification of methods includes (1) adversary (the articulation and resolution of conflict); (2) conciliatory (effecting cooperation through accommodation and
assimilation); (3) developmental (mobilizing individual and
societal resources); (4) facilitative-instructional (teaching
and supervision); (5) those which develop and test knowledge
(research, evaluation and the dissemination of findings); (6)
restorative (remedying impaired functioning); (7) regulatory
(encouraging adherence to rules and norms); (8) rule-implementing (operations and administrative functions); and (9)
rule-making (helping in the origination of policies and laws).
Bisno includes in his conceptualization of professional roles
such categories as service provider, advocate, marriage
counsellor, community developer, social planner, and mental health specialist. For the most part, these roles are
structure-related and too broad to use effectively in systems
analysis, but specific goals and tasks could be derived from
his categories.

Hearn[19] has supported Bisno's central theme of a
transactions focus; he sees the social worker functioning to
enhance the client's chances for success. In quoting William
Gordon, he says:

> Social work, (Gordon says), is matching something
> in person and situation, at any time and by any
> means, to help people wind up in situations where
> their capabilities are sufficiently matched with the
> situation to 'make a go of it. ' The problem then,
> is to define what is meant by 'making a go of it, '
> and to do so in a way that is compatible with the
> values of the profession.

But vested interests of agencies and professions may, at
times, limit success in achieving this goal of maximization.

Warren Bennis foresees the rising importance of
transactional roles in future efforts at welfare re-organiza-
tion. In the context of attempts to preserve some individu-
alism and basic rights for clients and professions,

> ... Bennis sketches the types of organizational
> arrangements that will be necessary to deal with
> the problems of the future. Basically, he sees
> five key developments emerging. First, organi-
> zational arrangements will become temporary

systems.   Second, organization will revolve around
the problem to be solved, and not any a priori
conception of human organization.   Third, problems will be solved in groups of relative strangers
who possess diverse professional skills.   Fourth,
linking personnel will be required to coordinate
the diverse activities of numerous problem-solving
groups within an organization.   And fifth, leadership will fall to those most able to solve problems, rather than to those who can play the organizational game. [20]

The Challenge to the Social Work Profession

The impact of technology upon theory, social systems
and functional personnel roles has been summarized.   What
is the message for social work?   It is clear that new roles,
the transactions focus, and the idea of flexible systems related to problem-solving, all indicate the need for a drastic
departure from the previous professional focus, which has
traditionally been on behavior changing and the individual's
personality system.   Increasing numbers of practitioners
and social work educators are revealing an awareness of the
need for change, but do we have the knowledge base and the
innovative capacity which are essential for constructive systems development, and for methodological adjustments to
changed structures?

We have called attention to the low preference for
social systems specialists in graduate social work faculties.
We might also have challenged the lack of insistence on
study in depth in the social sciences, in undergraduate social work curricula, and in the admission policies of graduate schools of social work (which frequently ask for very
little preparation in the social sciences, especially in economics and government).

There are also questions concerning the attitudes of
professional social workers towards change.   The findings
of research conducted by Pearman and Jahns[21] on the diffusion of the developmental role-task model (involving the
use of such roles as social broker, advocate, teacher and
mobilizer) provide some reasons for questioning the adaptability of professional social workers.   Questionnaires were
sent to 305 undergraduate social work instructors (some of
whom also had duties with graduate curricula), and the

general impression gained from 186 respondents was that instructors with the MSW-only were the most resistant to innovation.   Comparisons were made among those instructors
(1) without a master's degree in social work; (2) those with
an MSW; and (3) those with at least one year of graduate
study beyond the MSW.   In summary, the MSW's regarded
their family and educational backgrounds as being less conducive to the acceptance of new ideas than the other two
groups.   They were also less dissatisfied with traditional
social work methods--separate or integrated casework, group
work and community organization.   MSW-only respondents
were emphatic as to a good teacher's willingness to test a
new idea, but those in the other two groups who were informed about the developmental role-task model were twice
as likely to use it in instruction.   The MSW's were less
likely to see the model as adaptable to their present teaching position, and less certain that the social- and client-
system approaches were compatible.

     As is the case with other human beings threatened by
change, the reactions of professional social workers to cybernation, and to related systems changes, are likely to be
varied.   We can expect less emphasis on jobs with a direct
face-to-face and "behavior changing" focus, and a reduction
in the number of those whose function is worker-management
liaison.   Also, as has been indicated, invasion from related
academic areas is likely to increase.   These changes might
be readily accepted; or they could lead to (1) increased reliance on professional organizations or unions to reduce
competition, and facilitate bargaining with management; (2)
dishonesty and deceit, through competition in arenas where
political finesse outweighs professional skill and knowledge;
(3) recognition of change with reluctant conformity; or (4)
denial and avoidance.

     Our hope is for a more active formal and informal
role on the part of the social work profession in the establishment of accountability, and of dynamic change or "learning systems," in service programs.   Schon[22] and Rivlin[23]
have affirmed the efficiency of the centralized use of computers in making money payments, and the existence of a
demand for increased accountability in social work services.
Acquisition of more knowledge from the social sciences,
with special awareness of the impact of technological change,
is essential.   The structure, function and relationship of
larger systems and sub-systems must be accurately perceived.   Perhaps a final challenge is how the dedicated

social worker may acquire new theoretical knowledge, put it into operation within pertinent systems, and still retain feelings of self-respect and a positive self-identity.

Notes

1. See William F. Ogburn, On Culture and Social Change (Chicago, 1964).

2. Reece McGee, Social Disorganization in America (San Francisco, 1962), 19-22.

3. Richard P. Appelbaum, Theories of Social Change (Chicago, 1970), 65-117.

4. Donald A. Schon, Beyond the Stable State (London, 1971), 12.

5. Ibid., 31-9.

6. Donald N. Michael, Cybernation: The Silent Conquest (Santa Barbara, California, 1962), 13-14.

7. Donald A. Schon, Technology and Change: The New Heraclitus (New York, 1967), 8-42.

8. Peter M. Blau and W. Richard Scott, Formal Organizations (San Francisco, 1962), 27-40.

9. Allen Schick, "The Cybernetic State," Transaction, 7 (February 1970), 15-26.

10. John Kenneth Galbraith, American Capitalism (Cambridge, Mass., 1962), 108-54.

11. Sidney Fine, "A Systems Approach to Manpower Development in Human Services," Public Welfare, 28 (January 1970), 93.

12. Richard Onken, A Survey of Faculty in Graduate Schools of Social Work (New York, 1968), 25.

13. Gerald C. Smith, "Planning and Administrative Manpower for the Cities," Occupational Outlook Quarterly, 13 (Spring, 1969), unpaged reprint.

14. Joseph B. Bracy, in a speech on manpower needs in
     future income maintenance programs delivered at
     the 98th Annual Forum of the National Conference
     on Social Welfare, Dallas, Texas, May 1971.
     (Copies can be obtained from NCSW, 22 West Gay
     Street, Columbus, Ohio 43215.)

15. Such a danger may be far greater than that of repug-
     nant, authoritative administration in social welfare
     organizations. Complex bureaucracies, the potential
     of the computer, and other control devices, may
     combine to produce an elitist "Warfare, Welfare,
     Communications, Industrial, Police State" as de-
     scribed by Bertram Gross in "Friendly Fascism:
     A Model for America," Social Policy, 1 (November-
     December 1970), 48.

16. There have been several contributions to job analysis
     in social work. In addition to those of Sidney Fine,
     previously cited, there are the recent contributions
     of Eugene J. Koprowski, "A Dynamic Role-Centered
     Approach for Developing a Generic Baccalaureate
     Curriculum in the Helping Services," in Undergradu-
     ate Education and Manpower Utilization in the Help-
     ing Services, Western Interstate Commission on
     Higher Education (Denver, 1967), 1-11; and Max
     Siporin, "Social Treatment: A New-Old Helping
     Method," Social Work, 15 (July 1970), 13-26.

17. See Robert J. Teare and Harold L. McPheeters, Man-
     power Utilization in Public Welfare (Atlanta, Geor-
     gia: Southern Regional Education Board, 1970), 31-
     42.

18. Herbert Bisno, "A Theoretical Framework for Teach-
     ing Social Work Methods and Skills, with Particular
     Reference to Undergraduate Social Welfare Educa-
     tion," Journal of Education for Social Work, 5,
     (Fall, 1969), 5-19.

19. Gordon Hearn, (ed.), The General Systems Approach:
     Contributions Toward an Holistic Conception of So-
     cial Work (New York, 1969), 65.

20. Eugene Koprowski in "The State Personnel Administra-
     tor in Manpower Utilization in the Helping Services,"
     included in Dutton Teague and Dorothy Buck (eds.),

Utilization of Manpower in Mental Health and Related Areas (Boulder, Colorado: Western Interstate Commission for Higher Education, October 1968), 30-1.

21. J. R. Pearman and Irwin R. Jahns, of Florida State University, in a paper entitled "The Diffusion of an Innovative Methods Model into Course Content," presented at the 98th Annual Forum of NCSW, Dallas, Texas, May 1971. (Copies can be obtained from NCSW, 22 West Gay Street, Columbus, Ohio 43215.)

22. Donald A. Schon, Beyond the Stable State, op. cit., 116-80.

23. Alice M. Rivlin, Systematic Thinking for Social Action (Washington, D. C. , 1971), 1-144.

6. FOUR SOCIAL SCIENCE CONCEPTS
    RELATED TO SOCIAL WORK ROLES*

Bob Dylan, patriarch of rock music, wrote in a fa-
mous rock classic in 1966, "the times they are a-changing. "
While he did not indicate direction, he did allude to exponential change. It is just this exponential change which
confounds and compounds the actualization of social work
roles in 1972. The key phrase here is "actualization of social work roles. " Contrary to what George Wallace would
have you believe about "pointy head intellectuals and fat-cat
bureaucrats, " there is a continuous, linear vector of theory
to practice, hence roles. Webster gives one definition of
role as "a function assumed by someone--as an advisor
role. " More specifically, role has been described in such
terms as social broker, mobilizer, teacher, evaluator, and
advocate. In summary, our usage of "role" implies a transaction between the social worker and client and relevant
sub-systems involving a variety of tasks related directly or
indirectly to client behavior change or influence on systems
functioning in relation to client needs. It is to state the
obvious to say that in a complex and rapidly changing technological society, people who deal with problems of social
functioning must be well prepared in several social sciences.

The purpose of this chapter is to examine four social
science theories and sub-theories which would be useful in
the actualization of social work roles. The theories, which
will be summarized and correlated with social work roles,
are as follows: Power structure, systems orientation,
macro-economics as related to employment, and culture as
related to values and value interrelationships. These social science concepts are embedded in the following disciplines, respectively: sociology, political science, economics,
and anthropology. Before proceeding to each of the

*Published with permission of the co-author, Wayne Cissell,
B. S. W. , social worker, State Division of Family Services,
Jacksonville, Florida.

theory-concepts, it may be helpful to review reasons why
the subject of social science utilization is not as obvious as
it may seem on the surface. In other words, social work
as a discipline and profession has been reluctant to incorporate and apply social science theories. A summary of
our earlier, more lengthy discussion provides a frame of
reference.

This dearth of application is related to several factors. Social work's early and continuing preoccupation with
the psychoanalytic approach was not and is not conducive to
integration of several social science disciplines. It is a
somewhat narrow orientation with an emphasis on internal
causation of impaired social functioning. It stands to reason that if you accept the notion of the id, superego, ego,
and the subconscious, you will concentrate on therapies
which isolate the individual from environmental influences.
Cultural and societal vectors which are treated in various
social science disciplines will be ignored.

A second major factor is that social work is primarily concerned with actions and change. The social scientist aims at an accurate description of social work or
other social phenomena, and control is secondary. The
social worker is interested in controlling and guiding behavior while a social scientist seeks to explain social phenomena.

A third factor is the social work student's general
lack of expertise in social science areas. It amounts to
part of a vicious circle--undergraduates are often not required to take specific social science courses; on the job
they fail to apply that knowledge; this lack of application
completes the circle by making it seem that social science
expertise is not to be used or incorporated into curriculum.

So these three factors, as well as others previously
mentioned, have combined to separate theory and practice.
Discussion of the four theories will include: (1) elaboration
of the theories and concepts themselves, as well as (2) il-
lustrations of how knowledge of each concept will be useful
and "essential to effective practice."

The Power Concept

The concept of the structure of power, formal and

informal, has been treated in political science publications, but its basic theoretical framework is rooted in sociology. While each of these concepts is useful to several social work roles, power structure theory is especially close to the role of community organizer. Anyone who has tried to induce change knows that in addition to the formal, more or less representative echelons of power there is an "understructure" which can wield tremendous decision-making power. The force of this power is multiplied by the fact that this behind-the-scenes power is not necessarily accountable to anyone, except self-efficiency. In order to grapple effectively with any power structure, the community organizer and other practitioners must understand the informal aspects.

Four men are intimately connected with this theory: Floyd Hunter, Max Weber and C. Wright Mills are the theoreticians, while Saul Alinsky has made a career out of meeting the Power Structure head on. Floyd Hunter, in his study of "Regional City, " coined the term "power structure. " He found from an original list of 175 that in this city there were forty (40) men making policy and several hundred implementing it; i. e. , "The structure is that of a dominant policy-making group using the machinery of government as a bureaucracy for the attainment of certain goals coordinate with the interests of the policy-making groups. "[1] Of Hunter's forty leaders, the largest proportion, eleven, were heads of large commercial enterprises. Financial direction and supervision of banking and investment operations were represented by the next highest proportion, seven. Six professional people made the list; five lawyers and one dentist. Government had four, and labor, two. An interesting classification was "leisure personnel. " These people have leadership capacities but do not have business offices (e. g. philanthropists). [2]

The professional in "Regional City" appeared to be suffering from a case of "professional schizophrenia. " He was isolated from the upper echelons of power as well as being removed from the average citizen. However, Hunter did find that professionals tended to be more receptive to community problems. While the location of the men in power often tends to isolate them from, say, problems in the ghetto, very often the professional is in the middle of social problems:

Location tends to isolate men of power from the

mass of citizens less powerful than themselves
and from community problems. The professional
men take different routes from home to work.
Their way runs through an industrial and warehouse area. The store-fronts are painted in som-
bre colors which are smoke faded, giving the impression of dominant browns and grays. It is
true that the professional men turn into more
pleasant suburban streets at the end of their home-
ward journey, but most of the route is depressing
to anyone sensitive to social disorder. The smoke
pall, grassless yards, unwashed children rolling
abandoned automobile tires as hoops, gray dogs,
and the bargain clothing emporiums are constant
reminders of decisions which press for attention
on the leaders and their executors of power in the
community. [3]

Hunter's contribution to power structure theory can
be broken down into three major hypotheses highly related
to social work roles:

1.   The exercise of power is limited and directed
     by the formulation and extension of social policy
     within a framework of socially sanctioned author-
     ity.

2.   In a given power unit a larger number of indi-
     viduals will be found formulating and extending
     policy than those exercising power.

3.   In the realm of policy the top leaders are in
     substantial agreement most of the time on the
     big issues related to the ideology of the culture.

These hypotheses have direct implications and ramifications for social work roles. Students should study the
policy statements of the Committee for Economic Development in order to become acquainted with the liberal recommendations of enlightened elitists.

Max Weber was a major contributor to sociological
theory. Although he did not address himself specifically to
explaining the power structure concept, much of his work
on bureaucracies and social competition is applicable. Virtually every social worker has to contend with large bureaucracies. Most likely he is employed by a large bureaucracy,

and will at various times be called upon to confront a bureaucracy. Weber's idealized model of bureaucracy will
delineate some subtle dimensions which will help the social
worker:

1.   A hierarchical authority structure.
2.   Specialization in the division of labor.
3.   An impersonal approach to interpersonal rela-
     tions.
4.   "A priori rules."
5.   Separation of policy making and administration.
6.   Personnel assignment on basis of merit. [4]

Now this is an idealized approach; in actuality a bureaucracy may be quite different. However, these dimensions are applicable. Almost all formal and informal power
structures are hierarchical. While there is some specialization within the structure, most positions of equal status
are interchangeable. Relations among the elite tend to be
more personal than relations between the elite and persons
of lesser rank. Hunter found that many of "Regional Cities"
decisions were made over lunch or dinner. The power
structure is adept at separating policy-making and administration. Very often people with grievances do not understand this. They may put pressure on an official who ad-
ministers the unpopular policy, but really has no control
over repealing it.

Weber's work on competition in social relationships
is applicable to any worker who must confront power structures:

> A social relationship will be called a struggle in-
> sofar as the behavior of one party is oriented pur-
> posefully toward making his own will prevail
> against the resistance of other parties. If the
> means of such struggle do not consist in actual
> physical violence then the process is one of
> 'peaceful' struggle. This peaceful struggle will
> be called competition if it is carried on as a
> formally peaceful attempt to obtain control over
> opportunities and advantages which are also cov-
> eted by others. Competition will be known as
> 'controlled competition' if its means and ends are
> subject to the same authority. This frequently
> latent social or individual struggle for advantages
> and for survival, without being necessarily based

on a conflict of interests, will be called selection;
insofar as it is a question of the relative opportunities of individuals during their own lifetime, it
is a form of social selection; insofar as it concerns the varying probability of the survival of in-
herited characteristics, it is a form of biological
selection. [5]

C. Wright Mills is best known for his work on the
"power elite." His concept of power rests on the assumption that there is a national power structure other than the
formal, representative one.   He went one step further and
said what many members of the New Left are saying today--
not only is there a national behind-the-scenes power structure, but also elected officials are bought and manipulated
by it. [6] The power elite has three components: The military, big business, and political functionaries.   It operates
in much the same manner as Hunter's "Regional City" power
structure.   However, the stakes are much higher, and activity is on a broader scale.   The power elite has the capa-
bility of controlling all aspects of our society and they cor-
respond roughly to a ruling class.   Mills based his argument on the assumption that power, by its very nature, will
become concentrated.   Groups with countervailing power
will reach a point of cooperation and collusion. [7]   Hunter
refers to the top men in groups as follows:

> The structure of top number-one leaders tended
> toward closure.   The number-one men knew num-
> ber-one men.   They recruited rising number-one
> leaders into their orbit and excluded those who
> did not fit.   They knew generally the pattern of
> policy development, and they knew well and speci-
> fically how to go about getting what was good for
> them and their individual enterprises.   Their
> names appeared repeatedly in the national press.
> They knew and were known by elected and ap-
> pointed officials, from whom they tended to hold
> themselves somewhat superior and aloof. [8]

Perhaps the practitioner with the most experience in
confronting the power structure was Saul Alinsky.   Regardless of whether or not you accept his methods, it must be
recognized that he had much to offer the social worker.
Alinsky operated on the assumption that in order to effect
meaningful change, force must be met with force.   His idea
of a vehicle of change (force) would be a neighborhood

grass-roots organization which would confront the establishment. Alinsky did not waste time in esoteric discourses on
the nature of the power structure. It was sufficient for him
to know what departments of the structure are amenable to
grass-roots pressure. The problem for Alinsky was not
who makes policy, but how policy making power can be
transferred to peoples' organizations. [9]

There are advantages and disadvantages to this approach which the social worker should be cognizant of.
Some advantages are: conflict usually works; it may help
to sharpen issues and enable people to distinguish more
easily between two points of view; conflict can be a creative
force; it can get a seat at the bargaining table for the dis-
enfranchised, and it usually results in some shift in the
distribution of power. Some disadvantages are: it can be
just a temporary stimulus; when the single issue ceases to
be controversial the whole organization may collapse; there
may be conflict for the sake of conflict, and it may result
in the identification of the wrong enemy. [10]

The concept of a "Power Structure" has a great deal
of face validity for two social work roles especially--the
community organizer and the advocate. The community organizer and the advocate are constantly called upon to confront and interact with those segments of the community that
wield power. The following will be an attempt to analyze,
critique, and relate the power structure concept to those
two social work roles.

Perhaps the important thing for the social worker is
to conceptualize the power structure he is dealing with.
While discussion has concentrated on an elitist view, there
are other viewpoints. Robert Dahl is perhaps the most
articulate spokesman against the methodology used and the
conclusions reached in the Hunter analysis. He criticized
the "reputational method," used by Hunter, which consisted
of having prominent citizens relate who they thought were
the real leaders. He went on to attack the elitist view as
unscientific because its covert nature makes it impossible
to prove or disprove. "The least we can demand of any
ruling elite theory that purports to be more than a meta-
physical or polemical doctrine is, first, that the burden of
proof be on the proponents of the theory and not its critics,
and, second, that there be clear criteria according to which
the theory could be disproved. "[11] Dahl proposes a pluralistic view which assumes a non-monolithic power structure.

It is contended that both models have a certain amount
of validity, and the social worker would benefit by fitting a
model to his particular purpose and situation. If he is a
community organizer in the Alinsky mold, he will want to
sharpen issues by maintaining an elitist viewpoint. If he is
an advocate trying to get the best for a client, he may want
to assume a pluralistic stance, with emphasis perhaps on
playing off one force against another. He will work for the
least costly tradeoff.

Weber's model of bureaucracy will be useful for
several social work roles--advocacy, brokerage, community
organizer, etc. Using his idealized guide as a baseline,
the worker can compare formal and informal aspects of
structure. This will greatly expedite efforts to work within
a large bureaucracy. C. Wright Mills' concept of a national
elite might not be directly relevant to specific roles, but it
is important to ponder the implications of this theory for
national funding of social welfare programs. Hunter's formulations have many direct applications. Especially significant is his warning that pressure on a public official may
be a waste of time when that official is only implementing
policy made by someone behind the scenes. [12]

Systems Concepts of Political Scientists

Social work roles are related to the systems orientation approach in political science. Probably some sort of
systems approach has been tried for hundreds of years but
specific and scientific adaptations are of recent origin. [13]
Behaviorists in political science were among the first to
use it in an organized manner. Behaviorists focus on persons or groups rather than structures, institutions, ideol-
ogies, or events:

> Just as the more fundamental behavioral perspec-
> tives--like the interdisciplinary focus, the concern
> with conceptual clarity, the emphasis on empiri-
> cism--are distinct by-products of the changes in
> philosophy and social science in general, so too
> are certain specific innovations of behaviorism.
> One is the development of the systems analysis
> approach. Atomic theory stands as 'grand' or
> comprehensive theory in the physical sciences,
> and systems analysis is considered to be its
> analogue in social and political science. It tries

to depict social and political life as a system in
which all parts are regularly and functionally related, a kind of regular and self-consistent universe. Systems analysis sometimes tends to reflect the presumed scientific rigor of social scientists who believe that the first order of business
of science is the creation of precise conceptual
frameworks by which the variety of existence can
be explained. [14]

So the concept of systems approach has its roots in behaviorism. This is a logical conclusion since behaviorism has
always maintained a logical, empirical orientation.

It is clear from the above that the fundamental notion
in the systems approach is the concept of "system. " There
are probably several definitions of "system" but they all
agree in one respect. To speak of a system means to single out for attention first some population of elements or
entities, next some variables in terms of which the entities
are described, and finally some specified relations among
the variables. An important notion is the concept of "steady
states" or stable equilibrium. Stable equilibrium occurs
when accidental departure from equilibrium sets into motion
forces which bring the system back to equilibrium. A
stable equilibrium is characterized by negative feedbacks.
An unstable equilibrium occurs when accidental departures
set in motion forces that carry the system further and in
the same direction; it is characterized by positive feedback. [15]

A system is generally a set of objects together with
relationships between the objects and between their attributes. In order to assume that a system exists, one must
be able to specify elements and relationships which are essentially invariant. The boundaries between the system and
its environment must be defined. So the systems theorist
looks for rules which enable him to establish correspondence
between some aspect of nature and the structure of his
model. Two aspects of this approach make it attractive for
social scientists:

1. It is equally applicable to all aspects of nature,
    and
2. The progress of model formulation in views of
    observable events may be conducive to extrapola-
    tion to areas replete with non-observable events. [16]

Some other properties of political systems include the following:

1. It is assumed that they are adaptive, i. e. , they
   don't just react passively.
2. They may be subject to stress.
3. They have empirically discoverable life processes.
4. They have elements, or units.
5. They have members--individuals who perform
   political actions. [17]

It is clear from the above that systems orientation
is a highly scientific, logical stance. It is based on the
physical sciences, and adapted by the behaviorists While
there does exist a thought-action dichotomy between social
science and social work, systems theory is easily applicable.
The social worker should approach a problem as a mani-
festation of malfunctioning of a part of a sub-system. The
client's problem should be viewed in terms of his particular
position in the entire systems environment. Field theory
and the Gestalt view in psychology have accepted this viewpoint. The worker should be cognizant of the departures
from equilibrium. Other forces should be considered.
Workers should be familiar with the concepts of "homeo-
stasis, " shock, stress, feedback, and importation of energy.
If the social worker is to help the client, he must take into
account these concepts.

Macro-Concepts of Economics

The third major theory lies in the realm of econom-
ics--macro-economics and employment. Economics has
been defined in various ways, but the following is a neat
formulation of economic and related aspects, by Robert L.
Heilbroner. The economic "problem" can be viewed in
three ways:

1. A macro-approach emphasizing total processes
   and outputs.
2. A micro-approach roughly corresponding to systems analysis where units are analyzed and put
   into proper perspective.
3. A combination of the two with emphasis on evolutionary vertors.

Economics is the study of a universal human process providing for the physical well-being of society.   Economic
history focuses on how man solves the problem of survival.
It is a paradox that survival unaided is inversely related to
the richness of a nation.   There are two major economic
tasks for every society:

1. Organize a system to assure production of enough
    goods and services for its own survival, and
2. Arrange the distribution of the fruits of its pro-
    duction so that more production can take place. [18]

Volumes and volumes have been and will be written
on macro-economics and employment.   There are several
viewpoints of causation ranging from structural formulations
to individual motivation.   Space will permit presentation of
only a few views by some noted authorities on the subject.
Perhaps no other book did more to raise the level of awareness of the poverty problems in America than Michael Harrington's The Other America.   Among other things, he
spoke of two classes of marginal employables or rejects.
One class consisted of the unskilled, constantly moving from
job to job.   These are the dishwashers, the day laborers,
etc.   Another class consisted of those who were once considered skilled and on the way up, but are now down and
out due to technological unemployment.   Both classes make
up what Harrington labels the "economic underworld. "[19]
He saw the unemployed as victims of the economic system.

Charles Killingsworth argues for the existence of a
structural basis of unemployment.   The unemployment problem is not due to lagging aggregate demand, but is caused
by labor imbalance.   He cites figures to prove that unemployment at the bottom of the educational scale is generally
unresponsive to increases in demand for labor due to increases in aggregate demand because these jobs are being
eliminated or taken over by machines. [20]   He saw adequate
investment in retraining and improved labor market systems
as being corrective.

Robert F. Solow takes an opposite view.   His interpretation of the facts utilizes insufficient aggregate demand
to explain unemployment problems:

> What I have been trying to say is that among the
> reasons for favoring extensive labor market policy
> one can not legitimately count a belief that the

American economy has behaved badly in recent
years because of a creeping failure of adjustment
to new technology and new demands. That plausible sounding analysis simply will not stand up
under close examination. The corollary to this
conclusion is that to set up labor market policy
as an alternate to expansionary fiscal and monetary policy is a double mistake. It is a mistake,
first, because the immediate problem to be faced,
the weak economic performance of the last seven
years, is primarily a reflection of insufficient
aggregate demand and needs to be attacked in the
obvious way. It is a mistake, second, because
it is hopeless to expect labor market policy to
work successfully in a climate of general under-
employment. [21]

The implications of economic theory may not be clear
to undergraduates in social work and administrators of those
programs. This is the crux of the problem. Social work
undergraduate curricula have shied away from requiring
economics. Perhaps this is part of the vicious circle mentioned earlier: i. e. , faculty are usually incompetent in this
area; therefore, it would be grossly unfair and sadistic to
subject students to the rigors of this discipline. However,
the discerning student and faculty member should be im-
pressed with the systems view which involves economic perception and program planning and budgeting techniques.
Economic theory can be highly applicable to social work
roles. For example, an application from macro-economic
theory is the concept of "pseudo free-enterprise. " By
realizing that there is virtually no such thing as "free enterprise, " the social worker can use this as a departure
point to justify social welfare programs which seek to inter-
cede with the system for the purpose of more equitable distribution of wealth.

Culture as Related to Values and Value Interrelationships

When one thinks of anthropology, visions of Dr.
Leakey fumbling around Olduvai Gorge appear. But anthropology in recent years has developed several branches from
the original two--cultural and physical. These branches include: linguistics, social anthropology, ethnography, ethnol-
ogy, and primatology. The point is that anthropology today
is much more amenable to interdisciplinary exchange.

Cultural anthropology has the greatest implications for social work roles. Whether one is in a brokerage or behavior changing role, a knowledge of cultural differences is essential to understanding and predicting individual and group behavior.

Culture as a concept and tool is fully utilized by anthropology. It is culture that makes man human. Take it away and he is just another primate. While behaviorists and physiologists may shudder at this generalization, anthropologists believe in it. Among many definitions of culture, this one is perhaps all inclusive: culture is made up of all the socially learned behavior, mutual expectations, common understandings, and values an individual shares with others of his group. The emphasis is on the phrase "socially learned behavior." In order to have socially learned behavior an organism must make use of symbols to transfer knowledge. In this respect, language is the true common denominator of all cultures. The study of linguistics makes use of this concept to try to reduce all languages to structures guided by universal laws.

Anthropology provides a rationale for understanding and examples of the importance of a knowledge of values and value priorities to human behavior and professional, political, and client decision making. A social worker needs depth in understanding the needs and values of human beings in order to understand personality differences and achieve maximal levels of efficiency in behavior changing and system manipulation or mobilization roles. Planning in a systems format calls for careful analysis of values of client-consumers and decision makers as a prerequisite to stating goals and objectives.

Social systems are, at the root-level, an outgrowth of personal and social values as values determine social goals and priorities. Also, anthropologists predict and interpret human behavior in relation to carefully defined values. Personality patterns emerge from definitions of acceptable modes of striving toward fulfillment of socially approved goals. If myth and superstition underlie behavior and decision-making among clients in Appalachia, then social workers and professionals in other helping services must understand the myths and superstitions of Appalachian people. Sociology and anthropology sometimes overlap in contributions to the understanding of culture and human values, but anthropology has made a unique contribution in the

study of primitive societies and then the utilization of this
basic knowledge in understanding the impact of cultural
traits upon contemporary behavior.

Value conflicts present a major problem in social
work practice. Diverse cultural values combine with professional values to promote friction with groups of people
with different values and systems orientation. Donna L.
McLeod and Henry J. Meyer in "A Study of Values of Social
Workers,"[22] presented a list of conflict-ridden polarities.
The first-mentioned of each of the following presents the
position toward which the profession was thought to tend.

1. Individual Worth vs. Systems Goals. Self-fulfillment, worth and dignity rather than group or
   system goals have been favored by social workers.
2. Personal Liberty vs. Societal Control. Rights of
   self-determination of clients have been stressed
   in professional relationships, but some note considerable control of the patient under therapy.
3. Group Responsibility vs. Individual Responsibility.
   Social work holds that the group is responsible
   for the well-being of its members.
4. Security-satisfaction vs. Struggle, Suffering, and
   Denial. There is a professional conviction that
   human beings must find satisfaction of biological
   and culturally-induced needs to reach their maximum potential.
5. Relativism-Pragmatism vs. Absolutism-Sacred-
   ness. Social workers seek pragmatic solutions
   free from the constraints of rigid moralism.
6. Innovation-Change vs. Traditionalism. Although
   there is evidence of rigidity in practice methods,
   social workers are comparatively open to change
   in other systems and are more change-oriented
   than the public.
7. Diversity vs. Homogeneity. Social work practitioners are thought to have greater respect for
   individual differences than most other groups.
   The cognitive orientation of social workers concerning the nature of man stresses cultural
   causation of human behavior, that individual behavior is dependent on the group, and that each
   individual is unique and complex, thus making
   character judgment impossible from a few known
   facts.

Obviously the social worker can benefit by application of anthropological theory. Social workers must decide if there is a culture of poverty, or a cultural gap between, say, whites and blacks. If the worker does choose to recognize these differences, he can make use of anthropological theory in this area. Even if we assume that cultural differences in the United States are not as important as class differences, we still need to understand and respect differences. Anthropology courses would benefit the undergraduate social welfare major by demonstrating different approaches, such as the structural-functional and holistic viewpoints. These approaches would be especially useful in work with minority groups who have retained a great degree of geographical and social cohesiveness, such as Herbert Gans' Urban Villagers.

In summary, regardless of the historical reasons for the lack of exchange between social science and social work, it is rational to assume that social work could greatly benefit by that input. The four areas related are just partial applications. A more adequate application of social science theories should include discussions of quantitative approaches, new emphasis on environmental causation, and the tremendous impact of operant psychology. Suffice it to say that future social work majors must receive the benefits of a greatly increased application of social science theory to social work roles.

Notes

1. Floyd Hunter, Top Leadership U. S. A. Chapel Hill: University of North Carolina Press, 1959.

2. Ibid.

3. Ibid.

4. Max Weber, Essays in Sociology. New York: Oxford University Press, 1946.

5. Ibid.

6. C. Wright Mills, The Power Elite. New York: Oxford University Press, 1946.

7. Ibid.

8. Floyd Hunter, op. cit.

9. Saul Alinsky, Reveille for Radicals. Chicago: University of Chicago Press, 1946.

10. Lyle E. Schuller, Community Organization: Conflict and Reconciliation. Nashville: Abingdon Press, 1966.

11. Robert A. Dahl, "A Critique of the Ruling Elite Model," American Political Science Review, June 1958, pp. 463-69.

12. Further discussion of the principal power theories may be found in Robert Lineberry and Ira Sharkansky, Urban Politics and Public Policy. New York: Harper & Row, 1971, pp. 146-163.

13. See Ludwig von Bertalanffy, "The Theory of Open Systems in Physics and Biology," Science, 3, pp. 23-29.

14. Cyril Roseman, Dimensions of Political Analysis. Englewood Cliffs, New Jersey: Prentice-Hall Inc., 1966.

15. Edward H. Buehrig (ed.), Essays in Political Science. Bloomington: Indiana University Press, 1966.

16. Robert T. Holt, The Methodology of Comparative Research. New York: The Free Press, 1970.

17. Ibid.

18. Robert L. Heilbroner, The Making of Economic Society. Englewood Cliffs, New Jersey: Prentice-Hall Inc., 1968.

19. Michael Harrington, The Other America. Penguin Books, 1962.

20. Charles Killingsworth, "The Structural Basis of Unemployment," from hearings before subcommittee on employment and manpower, U.S. Senate, 88th Congress, 1st Session, September 20, 1963, Part 5.

21. Robert F. Solow, "Testing the Structural Hypothesis,"

Wicksell Lectures, held in Stockholm, April 14, 1964.

22.   See Edwin J. Thomas, editor, Behavioral Science for Social Workers.   New York: The Free Press, 1967, pp. 402-16 for a more complete treatment of the value orientation of social workers.

7. THE DIFFUSION OF AN INNOVATIVE METHODS MODEL INTO COURSE CONTENT*

We are a society with many personal and social problems. On the domestic scene alone, we are faced with the challenges of poverty, unemployment, ill health, pollution, illiteracy, campus and ghetto riots, drug addiction, alcoholism, mental illness, a rising crime rate, a rising venereal disease rate, and the general inability of the social system to deliver services which will enable all or most of us to enjoy a good life without seriously hampering the chances of others to meet the same objective. We see glaring needs for new policies, programs and helping methods which will have greater preventive and restorative impacts. The quality of human resources is equally, if not more important than the quality of physical resources in efforts to improve cost-benefit relationships.

Several studies indicate that investment in education has brought greater returns than investment in additional physical capital.[1] It is a logical assumption that social work also has a high investment return potential in tangible as well as in non-tangible terms. But there is a growing concern as to which social work methods inputs will bring greatest outputs. Traditional separation of casework, group work, and community organization methods or attempts to integrate related traditional concepts and principles have not satisfied many who would like to see social work address itself to the solution of a wider array of personal and social problems.

The most frequently discussed change is in the direction of a developmental role-task-performance model in a

*The co-author is Irwin R. Jahns, Associate Professor, Department of Adult Education, Florida State University. Reprinted by permission of the Council on Social Work Education from the Social Work Education Reporter, v. 21, no. 1 (April-May, 1972).

merged client-social systems frame which involves several approaches to problem solving. Such roles as outreach, broker, advocate, mobilizer, teacher and evaluator are being proposed to supplement the previously emphasized role of direct behavior changer. There are several studies which have supported the questioning of traditional social work methods.

Evaluative Research on Social Work Methods

Samples of the dissatisfaction with traditional methods with a client-system and behavior changing focus include:

1. Henry J. Meyer, Edgar F. Borgatta, and Wyatt G. Jones, used professional caseworker self-evaluations and supervisory evaluations to establish the degree of success of casework service to girls from lower class homes in comparison with a control group of similar backgrounds with no special service. The results were discouraging. The experimental group evidenced little improvement in social and personal adjustment as compared to those who received no special social work help. [2]

2. David Wallace further questioned the efficacy of existing professional methods. The Chemung study compared casework effectiveness in public assistance family relations and unity, individual behavior and adjustment, household practices, health conditions and practices, care and training of children, social activities, economic practices, relationship to the project worker, and use of community resources. Two trained (MSW) caseworkers gave professional services to an average caseload of 25 while the control group was staffed by regular public welfare (non-MSW) workers with average caseloads of 60. At the end of a two-year trial period, no statistically significant difference could be found between the demonstration and control groups. A post-study evaluation of methods yielded the opinion that the quality of casework was slightly above average for the experienced public assistance workers who handled the control group and that the professional social workers who worked with the demonstration group were slightly below average. [3]

3. Thomas Tissue reported on current dissatisfactions of some Old Age Assistance social workers. Questionnaires were distributed to 809 public assistance workers and there was a 76 percent return. Thirty-nine percent

were "definitely" or "probably" planning to leave their employment. Dissatisfaction was largely associated with inadequate training for the expected worker roles and with contradictory instructions from supervisors. Sixty-five percent of all respondents under age 30, and 51 percent of those over 30 thought that OAA clients would benefit more from increased grants than from increased service of the type they were getting. [4]

The Evolution of the Role-Task-Performance Model

The three examples mentioned above present a sample of the dissatisfaction with traditional methods of social work. Words such as "caseworker," "group worker," "community organizer," and "social actionist" do not adequately describe the helping activities of social workers which are needed to bring solution to problems. Consequently, several efforts have been exerted to provide a more exact definition of worker roles so that education may be geared to the effective performance of these roles. Contributors in this effort include:

1. Irving Weisman and Mary Baker used a critical incident method of job analysis in which they: (a) collected narrative descriptions of things done on the job which reflected the meeting of program aims, (b) abstracted actions or qualities which contributed to the effectiveness or ineffectiveness of the incident intervention, and (c) drew inferences as to the critical requirements for the job. [5]

2. Eugene J. Koprowski saw three major elements in a dynamic undergraduate curriculum-planning model: (a) that a helping services worker is trying to achieve occupational goals, (b) that these goals must be achieved within a system of constraints imposed by relevant social systems, and (c) that the vehicle for achieving these goals will be a series of dynamic interacting roles. The primary roles mentioned were: (a) change agent which involved teaching, counseling, supervising, disciplining, negotiating, arbitrating, and other related activities as they pertain to both client and social systems, (b) the administrative role, which involves gathering information, planning and writing reports, processing clients, interpreting policies, and keeping records, and (c) researcher, which involves the gathering, classification, and interpretation of data. [6]

3.   Herbert Bisno provided a sociologically-oriented framework for teaching social work methods.   His focus was on problems.   He interrelated the client system with other transactional systems.   Micro-system transactions included one-to-one and small group relationships.   Macro-system transactions included organizational and associational, intergroup and other large collectivities.   Methods discussed were adversary, conciliatory, developmental-facilitative-in-structional, knowledge development and testing, restorative, regulatory, rule-implementing, and rule-making.   He saw many roles, in addition to social caseworker, in which these methods can be applied.   He combined the new with the old when he mentioned provider-of-service, advocate, marriage counselor, community developer, social planner, community organizer, public welfare worker, child welfare worker, so-cial work teacher, court counselor, and mental health spe-cialist. [7]   Such role titles are, in part, structure-related and somewhat lacking in functional job descriptiveness.

4.   Max Siporin has incorporated social and client system methods.   He holds that the current interest in so-cial treatment indicates a return to the problem-person-situation model instead of the medical or symptom-illness view of social problems.   The gestalt was seen as including systemic, structural, functional and change characteristics. Change was related to the system and its inter-relationships rather than being an individual matter.   His view is me-chanistic in that it maintains that an interventive change in one element of the system may improve the functioning of the total system.   The social treatment approach would en-courage the use of a variety of interventive strategies and programs involving such roles as integrator and friend, problem-solving expert, broker, advocate, and teacher. [8]

5.   Robert J. Teare and Harold L. McPheeters led the development of one of the more meaningful models.   A developmental approach based on defined needs, rather than factoring out tasks for new job classifications, was used in the functional job analysis.   Nine major objectives of social work activity were determined to be: (a) detection of indi-vidual and group problems; (b) linkage with pertinent ser-vices; (c) advocacy, i. e. , fighting for the rights of clients; (d) mobilization, or utilizing existing groups, resources and organizations, or creating new ones to fill gaps; (e) instruc-tion--the imparting of helpful information; (f) behavior change or modification; (g) information processing and collection, classification, and analysis of data generated within the social

welfare environment; (h) administration or the management
of a facility, an organization, or a program, and continuing
care. The roles which were finally identified with illustrative tasks were outreach worker, broker, advocate, evaluator, teacher, behavior changer, mobilizer, consultant,
community planner, care giver, data manager, and administrator. [9]

Professionalization: A Catalyst or a Barrier to Innovation

Social work has sought to establish efficiency and
legitimacy through gaining professional recognition. But it
has been established that professionalization is not an unmixed blessing in furthering the goal of service effectiveness. In the earlier stages, at least, the introduction of
expertise and innovations, the improvement of skills through
more specialized training and better agency organization,
and the enticing of able personnel through more promising
career opportunities can bring great improvement in the
quality of services. But the values and problems of our
society change. Methodologies of the past become socially
latent and they do not necessarily meet the needs of the
present, and occupational self-interest accompanied by intra-
and inter-professional rivalries may act to deter change.
Martin Rein, among others, has contended that professionalization in the social services is a possible hazard to those
in greatest need because of the professional's striving for
prestige, the over-defining of skills, limitations on those
eligible to hold helping positions and increasing concern with
standards, personal satisfaction and income. [10]

The Innovation Diffusion Study

In light of evidences of dissatisfaction with traditional
social work methods and the mixed blessings of professionalization, we sought to discover the extent of diffusion of the
developmental-role-task performance model. We tried to
maintain a value-free approach while attempting to isolate
factors which were influencing stages of adoption from awareness to acceptance. Three questions were asked.

1) To what extent has the role performance model
become diffused throughout academic departments
offering undergraduate social welfare education?
2) To what extent have individual social welfare

instructors progressed from total ignorance of
this innovation to adoption?
3) What factors, if any, determine variation in the
diffusion and adoption of this innovation?

Questionnaires were sent to 305 undergraduate social
welfare instructors whose names appeared on lists furnished
by the Council on Social Work Education (209), Southern Regional Education Board (59), and the Western Interstate
Commission on Higher Education (37). We obtained a 62
percent return; 23 percent of the respondents were from
WICHE territory, 38 percent from SREB territory and 38
percent from the rest of the United States.

The Educational Variable[11]

Our questionnaire identified: 1) those undergraduate
instructors who had a master's degree in social work (N=
86); 2) those with a master's degree or above in fields other
than social work (N=33); 3) those with at least one year of
graduate study above the MSW (N=67). From this data we
were able to compare the MSW with a relatively high professional concentration with other undergraduate instructors.

As to general attitudes toward change, we found the
following differences among the 186 respondents.

1. Seventy-five respondents stated that family background was less than encouraging to the adoption of new
ideas, with 31 percent of the MSW's so reporting as compared to 18 percent of the MSW+ and 24 percent of the non-
MSW groups.

2. Education was viewed as positively stimulating to
the adoption of a new idea by 139 respondents, but only 67
percent of the MSW group gave this response as compared
to 82 percent of the MSW+ and non-MSW groups.

3. Thirty-seven respondents saw traditional social
work methods as being inappropriate, but only 17 percent of
the MSW's thought so, as compared to 25 percent of the
MSW+ and 23 percent of the non-MSW groups. A backup
question yielded that 18 percent of the MSW's, 43 percent of
the MSW+ and 19 percent of the non-MSW's were dissatisfied
with traditional social work methods approaches.

4. One hundred seventy respondents indicated that a good teacher would be willing to test a new idea or instructional model without waiting for others. Ninety-five percent of the MSW group gave this response.

Adoption of Role Task Model

As to the developmental role-task model, 71 of 186 respondents professed a thorough knowledge of it. Thirty-three of them had investigated but not tried it, while 38 had tried this model and were continuing to use it. But only 33 percent of the knowledgeable MSW's had tried the model as compared to 78 percent of the MSW+ and 66 percent of the non-MSW groups. Thirty-eight knowers saw unqualified adaptability of the role-task model in their current teaching position, while 26 percent of the MSW, 71 percent of the MSW+ and 50 percent of the non-MSW groups gave this response. Twenty-two knowers saw role-task social systems content as being obviously compatible with client system content, with 20 percent of the MSW group holding this view as compared to 50 percent of the MSW+ group. The question as to whether financial aid inputs were more important than service inputs was not found to be statistically significant but 16 percent of the MSW, 24 percent of the MSW+ and 14 percent of the non-MSW groups held this view.

The Location Variable

As to territory of residence, role-task performance responses varied as follows: SREB territory, 45 percent of the respondents professed knowledge of the model, with 44 percent of the knowers being adopters; WICHE territory, 31 percent of the respondents professed knowledge of the model, with 45 percent of the knowers being adopters; the rest of the United States, 36 percent of the respondents professed knowledge, with 67 percent being adopters. On unqualified adaptability of the role-task model in the current teaching position affirmative responses were SREB, 42 percent; WICHE, 61 percent; and the rest of the United States, 69 percent. On role-task social system content being obviously compatible with client system content: in SREB, 22 percent; in WICHE, 54 percent; and in the rest of the United States, 36 percent were in positive agreement. On financial aid being more helpful than services, respondent affirmative responses were as follows: SREB, 9 percent; WICHE, 20 percent; and the rest of the United States, 19 percent.

Conclusions on Receptiveness to Innovation

There is a strong but not conclusive suggestion that the MSW group was less innovative than the other two groups. A related suggestion is that professionalism, to the degree that it is related to direct practioner education, may have produced somewhat more conservative instructors than did other educational patterns. In summary, the MSW's viewed their family and educational backgrounds as being less stimulating toward the acceptance of new ideas than did the other groups. Also, they were less dissatisfied with traditional social work methods. Although the MSW respondents were emphatic as to a good teacher's willingness to test a new idea, the knowers in the other groups were twice as likely to try the developmental role-task model. The MSW respondents were less likely to see the model as adaptable in their present teaching position and less certain that the social system and client system approaches were compatible. In the face of national policy swing toward financial aid in a tradeoff with services, relatively few respondents favored this input preference, with the MSW group taking a middle road.

Factors other than education may explain the differences which we have described, but other cross tabulations were of limited statistical significance. There were some differences in our three regions, with the SREB area being the most conservative, but this difference may be largely related to educational backgrounds, since 55 percent of the SREB respondents were in the MSW group as compared to 40 percent in WICHE territory and 41 percent in the rest of the United States. Our findings do not contradict current social work education policy that a person with an MSW teaches methods courses, but there is evidence that an MSW+ or doctorate will probably bring greater innovativeness and willingness to adjust to social change and social needs.

Notes

1.   Thomas I. Ribich, Education and Poverty (Washington: The Brookings Institution, 1968), pp. 8-14.

2.   Henry J. Meyer, Edgar F. Borgatta, and Wyatt G.
     Jones, Girls At Vocational High: An Experiment in
     Social Intervention (New York: Russell Sage Founda-
     tion, 1965).

3.   David Wallace, "The Chemung County Evaluation of
     Casework Services to Dependent Multiproblem Fam-
     ilies," Social Service Review, XLI, no. 4 (1967),
     pp. 379-384.

4.   Thomas Tissue, "Expected Turnover Among Old-Age
     Assistance Social Workers," Welfare In Review,
     VIII, no. 3 (1970), pp. 1-7.

5.   Irving Weisman and Mary Baker, Education For Social
     Workers in the Public Welfare Services, The Cur-
     riculum Study, Vol. VII (New York: Council on So-
     cial Work Education, 1959).

6.   Eugene J. Koprowski, "A Dynamic Role-Centered Ap-
     proach for Developing a Generic Baccalaureate
     Curriculum in the Helping Services," Undergraduate
     Education and Manpower Utilization in the Helping
     Services (Denver: Western Interstate Commission
     on Higher Education, December, 1967).

7.   Herbert Bisno, "A Theoretical Framework for Teach-
     ing Social Work Methods and Skills, with Particular
     Reference to Undergraduate Social Welfare Educa-
     tion," Journal of Education for Social Work, V.,
     no. 1 (Fall, 1969), pp. 5-17.

8.   Max Siporin, "Social Treatment: A New-Old Helping
     Method," Social Work, XV, no. 3 (1970), pp. 13-
     26.

9.   Robert J. Teare and Harold L. McPheeters, Manpower
     Utilization in Social Welfare (Atlanta: Southern Re-
     gional Education Board, 1970).

10. See Harry Gold and Frank R. Scarpitti, Combatting
     Social Problems: Techniques of Intervention (New
     York: Holt, Rinehart and Winston, 1967), pp. 523-
     24.

11. Greater detail as to comparisons of undergraduate in-
     structors under the educational variable is contained

in a paper, "Some Comparative Profiles of Undergraduate Social Welfare Educators, " by J. R.
Pearman, Irwin R. Jahns, and Ernest G. Gendron
Arete, 22 (Fall, 1972), pp. 77-95.   Also, Ernest
G. Gendron, "Relationships of Selected Factors Affecting Adult Basic Education Teachers, Innovativeness and the Diffusion of Educational Innovation, "
an unpublished dissertation, (Tallahassee: Florida
State University, 1970).

PART III

SOME APPLICATIONS OF SOCIAL SCIENCE IN SOCIAL WORK AND RELATED HELPING SERVICES

Part III broadens the scope of the integration of a generic social science core into the methodologies of social work-related and social work professions which logically employ such work performance roles as planner, social broker, educator, advocate, data manager, systems analyzer, and social planner. Knowledge concerning related professions, their progress in the utilization of social science knowledge and techniques, and information which they have generated in their helping efforts is mutually re-enforcing.

In a broad social welfare context, the failure to solve effectively the problem of poverty is discussed in terms of value and system constraints, the dualism and fragmentation of income maintenance programs, power inequities, welfare system weakness, and possible strategies for improving anti-poverty weapons. Adult education objectives and techniques are illustrated in a discussion of an aging program which would utilize economics content to aid public understanding and, especially, assist the aged in meeting some of their disadvantages in the market place and before governmental agencies.

An area of knowledge of growing importance to front-line workers in public agencies concerns laws and the legal system. In a follow-up survey of 1971-72 bachelor of social work alumni of Florida State University, 81 percent of those who had found social work positions reported their knowledge of welfare laws and court procedures affecting clients to be

inadequate, and 27 percent of the respondents regarded their
preparation as very inadequate.   A chapter on the legal system highlights inequities and trends toward and away from
entitlement and due process for welfare clients.   The position of the poor, in general, in their relationships with juvenile court procedures, bail bonding practices, and control
devices through procedural discrimination is discussed.

Medical information is essential to the effective performance of social work roles.   The 1972 survey of BSW
alumni showed that graduates who found social work positions
regarded the medical information which they had obtained in
their course work to be inadequate (88 percent) or very inadequate (50 percent). Knowledge of a study approach called
epidemiology, which describes the determinants and distribution of disease, crime, and other personal maladjustments,
is helpful in such roles as community planner and mobilizer.
The use of epidemiological principles, including the use of
demographic data, is included in a chapter on unmet medical
needs of children.   Additional information on epidemiology
methods can be obtained from such sources as Brian Mac-
Mahon, et al., Epidemiological Methods (Boston: Little,
Brown, 1960).   Helping service practitioners also need sufficient knowledge of diseases to communicate intelligently with
medical consultants and make proper brokerage arrangements.
A helpful handbook for this purpose is Community Research
Associates (Malvin Morton, editor), Chronic Disease: a
Handbook for Public Welfare Workers (Chicago: American
Public Welfare Association, 1966).

The restructuring of social services through a systems approach is illustrated by the example of a voucher day-
care system.   The final chapter describes some probable
impacts of the emerging limited growth economy upon social
work and related helping professions.   Such predictions may
seem to be somewhat devoid of rationality, but cybernetics
and related techniques have increased the reliability potential
of prediction.   Exploratory forecasting starts with today's
knowledge and works toward the future.   Normative forecasting starts with an assessment of future goals, needs and
desires and works back to the present.   A set of logically
conceived scenarios may also prove useful to planning.   Despite systems limitations, it might be empirically appropriate to state that the helping professions need to find techniques for prediction and planning in addition to "brainstorm-
ing. "

8. THEORY AND POWER INFLUENCES IN POVERTY-RELATED POLICIES*

Economic security programs have become important functions of government in industrialized areas because of certain related conditions. Primarily, difficulties in meeting basic needs give rise to circumstances of financial and emotional insecurity. Consequently, the individual faces many disappointments and frustrations in his effort to wrest satisfaction of his desires from limited natural and social resources. His total needs may not be met adequately even though material income appears to be sufficient, because some emotional and spiritual needs can not be met by material income alone. But a minimum income is generally regarded as a necessary condition for "happiness." Secondary aims, such as compensatory payment for risk-taking of veterans, or stimulation of material production, may also serve as justifications for welfare programs. Certain convictions concerning human motivation and the morality of receiving transfer payments, coupled with relative power positions of people, effect limits on poverty-reducing payments.

Limiting Institutional Forces

Our basic theoretical capitalistic system makes no provision for those who are outside the labor market either because they have no, or very low, productivity or because they can find no market for their limited capacity to render service and are, therefore, not considered available for employment. Other systems, such as the family, community mutual aid, and religion have met some needs. We have become increasingly aware of the limitations of our capitalistic model and we have compensated for these failures through public and private transfer payments. In addition,

*Reprinted with the permission of the co-author, Allen L. Pearman, and of Ball State University, from Indiana Social Studies Quarterly, v. 25, no. 3 (Winter, 1972-73). pp. 19-31.

some governmental and philanthropic activities serve to increase productivity and enhance economic growth, indirectly
improving living conditions of the poor through increased employment or by supplying greater amounts of goods and services per capita. But our version of capitalism retains the
basic productivity basis for income distribution, with the
poor and unorganized workers frequently finding themselves
in weaker and weaker market positions, both in acquiring
income and in purchasing goods and services.

     Institutional power positions influence the level of
transfers to the poor. In spite of our commitment to "minimum adequacy," our efforts to reduce or eliminate poverty
have been checked by some major competing forces. Social
deviations from the capitalistic model may be harmful as
well as helpful. Our economic system is greatly influenced
by bureaucratic social organizations which limit competition
and provide uneven benefits. Giant corporations, strong
labor unions, and a strong military establishment with non-
competitive procurement policies shift income away from the
more competitive elements. Inflation erodes the limited income of the poor and inflation control devices frequently
punish marginal workers and small, competitive firms severely.

Objectives of Public Assistance and Social Insurance Transfers

     Our motivations are mixed. Admittedly, we do not
make governmental transfer payments for the sole purpose of
eliminating poverty, but it is legitimate to look at program
impact from the poverty-elimination goal. Such particulari-
zation is essential to cost-benefit analysis, even though we
may wish to assess the total effect of existing income maintenance programs. It is also important that we look at historic and present values, because it is from the existing
complex of values that program and policy objectives are
formulated.

     Religious and philanthropic endeavors have served
conflicting purposes. Christianity had a strong commitment
to helping the needy. Reference to loving one's neighbor
and the spiritual rewards of giving are frequent in Christian
literature. These interpretations are not new, but application has varied. During the Middle Ages church canonists
did not regard poverty as a crime and they saw the poor as
honorable persons. Aid was dispensed with objectivity and

compassion in providing an acceptable level of adequacy at
the existing level of economic activity.   Later, the Eliza-
bethan Poor Law was not as vicious and inadequate as was
thought by welfare reformers of this century.   Recent research has revealed that private philanthropy stepped in to
continue more benign welfare practices than the public system provided.   In fact, records show that public funds made
up approximately seven percent of total welfare payments for
a forty-year period following the passage of Elizabeth 1601.[1]
But nonsectarian thinking about poverty was not consistent.
Calvinism brought impetus to the growth of capitalism by
encouraging frugality and material accumulation, but the
negative backlash was that the dependent person came to be
regarded as being morally inadequate because he was needy.
Private philanthropy mixed control of the poor with human-
itarianism.   Conformity was frequently the price of aid and
welfare policy changes were motivated, at least in part, by
fear of the restless poor.

    In the United States we have now moved to a predomi-
nantly secularized welfare system with a continuance of diverse and sometimes conflicting objectives.   Consequently,
goals are either unclear or inadequately met, or both.   We
revere the "earned right" principle inherent in social insurance because it fits the Protestant Ethic, even though our
poverty control impact is weakened thereby.   We enact laws
in the direction of the strongest political power instead of
focusing on the abolition of poverty and hunger.   Gaining
personal and party political power through responding to the
larger and more vocal constituent groups has brought greater
transfers to those above the poverty line than to those below it.   The agricultural aid program is a good example.
Payments are based on production and prices rather than on
the level of income.   Eight percent of total price-support
payments go to farmers whose average annual cash income
is $9,500.   The remaining twenty percent goes to 2.5 mil-
lion poor farmers.[2]   Meanwhile, we have bountiful docu-
mentation of the plight of migrant labor and the frequent
existence of hunger in the United States.[3]   Power considerations are apt to prevail over more humane Christian values
and the more generous theoretical viewpoints in non-market
income distribution manipulations.   Results might be stated
in the somewhat exaggerated terms that we have achieved
socialism for the rich and free enterprise for the poor.   Or
in adding the sinister-purpose possibility to the inadequate
result for the poor, Bertram Gross sees transfer payments
as a control device in maintaining elitist control in a

"Warfare, Welfare, Industrial, Communication, Police State. "[4]

The Governmental Budget Priority Position of the Poor

Individuals who are caught in the poverty trap are most unfortunate. We have not used our growing economic potential effectively in fighting poverty. We spent approximately 80 billion dollars through our public income maintenance programs in 1972, as compared to 29.9 billion dollars in 1960, but much poverty still exists.

Historically, we have been slow and selective in our efforts to meet basic needs through assistance and social insurance programs. Sometimes we appear to be losing ground. In terms of constant dollars and a $3,000 (now $4,300) poverty line, the number of poor families with no wage earner increased by 54 percent between 1947 and 1962, while the percentage of all poor families with this characteristic rose from 16 to 30 percent. During this same period, the number of all poor families fell 22 percent. [5] Social welfare expenditures, in general, have responded only moderately to national income capabilities. Public expenditures for social insurance, public assistance, veterans' programs, and health and medical services were 6.6 percent of the gross national product in the fiscal year 1934-35 and 9 percent in 1967-68. But all public expenditures grew from 20 percent to 32 percent of the gross national product during the same period. [6]

The social insurance and public assistance programs have a limited impact on poverty. In 1968, social insurance benefits were keeping approximately 3.6 million of 13 million recipient households above the poverty line. [7] The restrictiveness of the means test programs is evidenced by the fact that only 8,490,000 of approximately 30,000,000 persons living in poverty were receiving public assistance in August 1968. [8] In June 1972 about 55 percent of the poor were receiving some, although inadequate, public assistance. [9] If all public income payments are considered, 55.2 percent of 19.5 million recipient households were poor before receiving payments and 31 percent were poor after receiving payments in 1966. [10]

Dualism in the Rationale for Poverty Expenditures

Our basic justification for effecting social insurance
and public assistance transfers is need. Existent or probable economic dependency is presumed on the grounds that
the aged (with a minimum qualifying experience in the labor
market), the veteran, the unemployed, the injured worker,
and the Medicare recipient need and deserve income support.
Somewhat less fortunate are categories of the poor who must
demonstrate their need through some kind of means test.

The means test assumes definability of elements that
will make up a minimum budget to provide some prejudged
level of living. If this task is accomplished generously,
and seldom is this the case, then the system is still subject
to legislative willingness to provide money to pay one hundred percent of budgetary need. In 1958, states paid an
average of 94. 6 percent of budgetary need for Aid to Families of Dependent Children in the United States. [11] In early
1969 South Carolina was paying 54 percent of a standard
budget of $2,064 for a family of four under AFDC. [12] In
December 1972 Florida was paying 65 percent and Texas 75
percent of their budgets for AFDC cases.

We make an inconsistent application of presumptive
and demonstrated need in our fragmented and complex income
maintenance system and we compound the problem by taxing
the poor heavily. Government tax collections absorb about
one-third of the earned income of the very poor families. [13]
At the other extreme we presume that oil well owners deserve a 22 percent depletion allowance which can be applied
up to 50 percent of the total income.

The question arises as to why our basic theoretical
guidelines have not produced more adequate results. An
examination of the demonstrated and presumptive need concepts may further reveal their faults and point the way to
some logical solutions.

Demonstrated Need--The Means Test

Part of the answer to why we have inadequacy in welfare payments despite great growth in per capita income is
to be found in long-standing philosophical beliefs concerning
negative welfare effects if adequate help is provided for the
needy. Poor law limitations were possibly somewhat less

hampering in the agricultural primary group society, in which mutual aid and other forms of private philanthropy frequently met needs when disaster struck at the security of one of the "worthy" families in the community.   However, in an increasingly industrialized society poor law methods simply could not alleviate economic distress.   Increasing numbers of those considered "worthy, " as well as those with less condoned behavior records, came to need help.   Yet the basic poor law attitudes changed slowly.   Vestigial reminders of these poor laws still exist.   To understand properly the attitudes and methods associated with poor law measures, it is necessary to examine some of the psychological concepts underlying them.   Fear of the consequences of adequate public assistance is rooted in eighteenth-century concepts of the psychology of economic behavior.

Genesis of Classical Liberalism

Classical or laissez-faire liberalism grew out of a revolt against the controls of the medieval guilds over production and trade, and the "just price" and usury controls of the Roman Catholic Church.   It was also a response to the inhibiting doctrine of mercantilism; i. e., the idea that business existed to promote the power of the state and that inflow of precious metals was essential to the prosperity and power of the nation.   Adam Smith and other classical economists were opposed to interference with economic activity by the state because they feared that the advantages of economic specialization and automatic market adjustment would be impaired.

Merchants sought freedom from restrictions of government, guilds, or trade associations which might influence their economic choices.   With the advent of the industrial revolution, the world of commerce needed a philosophy proving that its newly found independence was not only for its own good but also unquestionably for the benefit of society. Business found this support in certain philosophical views (about human nature) which were originated in the seventeenth and eighteenth centuries.

Infused with the religious concept of stewardship, people believed that the "good person" would prosper materially; therefore, if the individual applying for relief was not able to support himself, he was wicked for not having used his time and abilities to prosperous advantage.   Only limited

relief was thus given because of the fear of rewarding evil
and destroying economic incentive to do better.

Advocates of limited and punitive methods of caring
for the needy thought that society was best served by applying the principles of a hedonistic philosophy, which provided
the rationale of poor law practices originated more than 350
years ago. Hedonistic views were augmented by other philosophical beliefs as to the nature of economic man, a concept central to classical economic incentive to do better.

Psychological Views of Classical Liberals[14]

There are four psychological premises underlying
classical liberalism--egoism, intellectualism, quietism, and
atomism. Hobbes, the exponent of egoism, saw man primarily as a self-seeking being acting in accordance with the
presumed laws of his biological nature. Even pity was regarded as an action motivated by the egoistic reaction, "I
might be in that predicament myself someday." Egoism is
one of the concepts underlying the philosophy of hedonism.

Jeremy Bentham qualified this concept of the pleasure-
seeking nature of man by maintaining that man's choices were
the result of an intellectual process essentially free of emo-
tion.

Quietism, the third point in the psychological creed
of the classical liberal, involved the notion that labor in itself is not pleasurable, but only a means to the end-desire
of pleasure. It held that thinking activities do not stimulate
desires, but rather that desires generate activity. Robert
Malthus, who believed that starvation was inevitable because
population tended to outrun food supply, would not recommend
newly-invented birth-control methods as a check on population
growth. He regarded marriage and the birth of children as
an absolutely necessary stimulus to industry on the part of
the individual.

Such hedonistic conviction as that expressed by Malthus still persists among many people in contemporary American communities. Some people say that man would not do
an hour's work if he did not have to in order to subsist.
The fallacy of this conclusion is obvious in many contemporary husband-wife families with no dependents in which both
work very hard to obtain an income far in excess of

subsistence. The classical conviction as to the disutility of
work and the utility of leisure carries the weakness of all
particularistic explanations of human behavior. Motivation
for work springs from many forces in addition to dire need,
and a large family does not guarantee effective work motivation on the part of the head.

The fourth view of the thinkers supporting the concepts of classical liberalism was a form of atomism. Total
behavior of any complex entity was regarded as a sum of
the behavior of its parts. The parts are viewed as having
an essential character quite independent from their relation
with each other. The atomist thinks of the whole society as
an aggregate of many individuals, isolated human units which
acquire no character from fellow units. This view contrasts
with the organic or holistic view that the whole society is a
multicellular organism in which a single unit (the cell, or
human being) loses its identity when separated from the
whole. It is erroneous to judge group behavior as a simple
additive of individual behavior. Individual motivation is not
standardized and the group has unique motivational characteristics.

Present Day Reflections of Eighteenth Century Concepts

One needs only to examine current public assistance
to see how generalized applications of hedonism have produced inequities. The defect is enlarged if the recipients
have weak political bargaining power, as we can plainly see
in the case of payments for Aid to Families of Dependent
Children.

In fact, we insist on such severe application of demonstrated need in the public assistance categories that we
end up with a system which perpetuates poverty. For example, in June 1972, the monthly payments to beneficiaries
in the United States were as follows: Old Age Assistance,
$78.12 average, with a range among the states from South
Carolina's $48.93 to $167.32 in New Hampshire; Aid to the
Blind, a $108.04 average, with a range from $67.19 in
South Carolina to $170.64 in Alaska; Aid to the Permanently
and Totally Disabled, a $99.85 average, with a range from
$56.55 in Louisiana to $168.58 in Alaska, and Aid to Families of Dependent Children, $52.16 average, with a range
from $14.72 in Mississippi to $97.85 in Massachusetts.
State-county financed general assistance averaged $67.42 and

ranged from $5.83 in Arkansas to $134.11 in New Jersey.
Several states, such as Florida, having no statewide program of general assistance reported no statewide averages.
Only 1.8 percent of personal income went into public assistance programs in 1972.

One need not document the numerous expressions of
classical liberalism by the categorical assistance programs.
We (1) are afraid that minimumly adequate welfare payments
will invite too many to the rolls, (2) are even more afraid
that aiding those in the work force will discourage interest
in (un)available jobs, (3) try to push welfare clients into
training for non-existent jobs, (4) sanction a higher level of
living for welfare clients who do some work than for those
who are unable to work, and (5) favor some physically limited categories, e.g., the blind over others through special
rehabilitation programs and higher assistance payments.
Part of the advantage of the blind is explainable in terms of
successful organization and lobbying efforts. [15]

Gradually we have made selective departures from a
poor law philosophy. We have admitted that causes of income insufficiency may be fortuitous or social. Consequently, we have come to view losses resulting from certain fundamental risks as partially compensable. Some modern social thinkers, in attempting to apply their knowledge in the
direction of maximization of human satisfaction, look at government as a tool which may be used to increase rather
than diminish human welfare. We have presumed need for
retired, aged workers and their survivors under the Social
Security Acts. Being unemployed, a veteran, or a farmer
has justified preferential treatment without means test restrictions. Presumptive need policy has rested largely on
the conviction that some dependent categories are more deserving than others or that payments to these groups will
benefit the total economy or enhance individual and party
political fortunes. Programs which are based on presumptive need are costly since payments are made at all income
levels. Consequently, from 60 to 70 percent of the benefits
go to persons above the poverty line.

The Power Factor

The authors have made reference to power forces
throughout this chapter even though we have focused on other
values and motivations relative to attitudes toward poverty

and helping programs.   Admittedly, those desiring power
may select the values and motivational theories which
strengthen their case.   But there is another dimension.
There is a growing awareness of the central importance of
power and conflict on the part of both social change theorists
and social actionists.

Conflict theory of social change is replacing equilibrium which involves a self-correcting force within a unitary
system, as described by Homans, Parsons, Brown and others.   Equilibrium is a central concept of classical economics.
Essentially, the equilibrium theorists took the functionalist
viewpoint, i. e. , that the total social system is a unit and
that selective, mechanistic change would be more disruptive
than helpful in the solution of social problems.   Hence the
conservatism of the equilibrium theorist.   But there is a
growing question as to the justice and maximization of welfare potential of this supposedly impartial and self-regulating
social system.   The original Marxist challenge has been re-
placed by non-revolutionary conflict theorists such as Coser,
Dahrendorf, Boulding, Kerr, and others. [16]

A current conflict theorist, Raymond Mack, believes
that power is a central concept of social science and that an
understanding of conflict is an essential requirement for the
understanding of social change and social problems.   Mack
holds that conflict is as inevitable as social organization,
but that we neglect the study of conflict and the importance
of power in the effort to understand how human needs are
being met.   There is a scarcity of resources and power
positions and a variation in the abilities of people who wish
to acquire these material and non-material rewards.   Conflict ensues and the expression of power generates opposition.   Subcultures arise and countervailing strategies are
developed.   Solidarity is fostered by attacks on the opposing
group.   As the complexities of society increase, so do the
problems and frustrations. [17]   Disadvantaged groups vie for
power as reflected in the tactic of acquisition of power and
the promotion of controlled conflict as the central means of
improving the living condition of the poor and disadvantaged.
Warren Haggstrom, among others, sees this polarization and
client-participation as essential to constructive social change. [18]
Such a conflict-oriented dialectical process can benefit special groups and, possibly, improve living conditions in society as a whole, but individual character assassination, de-
struction of positive, liberal change groups, and loss of life
or property may become costly in the absence of adequate

restraints.

The Welfare Rights Movement and urban riots suggest
that society can no longer effectively insulate the power of
the alienated poor and other disadvantaged groups. It may
be argued that abolition of poverty by insuring some minimum
income would remove one of the causes of crime, disease,
and other current problems, thereby helping us to isolate
and cost the removal or reduction of other causes. Basic
social welfare guidelines which would provide equity, fully
consider needs, and adequately weigh the social impact
should provide a catalyzing effect in other reform efforts.
In a concluding statement on influence and social change,
William Gamson states:

> Social change may also occur through conscious,
> explicit decisions which alter the social structure.
> Laws are an example of such decisions. One
> might well argue that the major thrust of social
> change in the United States has been to subject
> more and more forces to the manipulation of con-
> scious decision. Many forces which were taken
> as 'given,' as the uncontrollable set of limiting
> conditions for decisions, are now regarded as in
> part manipulable. This is nowhere clearer than
> in the economic realm where such things as fluc-
> tuations in the business cycle, growth rate, price
> stability, unemployment, and many other economic
> factors used to be regarded as the inexorable facts
> of life within which a government must work.
> Now, these forces have become the subject of con-
> scious economic policy. The control is not com-
> plete, of course, but these forces are regulated
> and harnessed for certain ends.19

Power is a central social phenomenon and conflict is
characteristic of social change. But conflict must be contained and institutionalized to avert misery, death, and the
loss of property. Social welfare theorists can assist by
helping to establish guidelines for guaranteed minimum income and for a system which provides like treatment for
those with similar needs. Such a system should also include
readily accessible avenues for groups of clients to verbalize
their needs and seek redress of their grievances.

The Inequities and Inefficiency of Categorical Aid

It is rather clear that our complex income maintenance programs based on demonstrated or presumptive need
are ineffective in bringing families and individuals up to the
poverty line of $4,300 for the typical family of four. In
general, payments under both approaches are too low to provide effective weapons against poverty. The dualism of the
system clouds the poverty issue. People become very concerned when they hear that about eighty billion dollars were
paid out in social welfare expenditures during the fiscal year
1972 by all levels of government, and they react very strongly against the assistance program clients, especially those
receiving AFDC benefits. But only sixteen billion dollars
(less than two percent of the net national product) was paid
out under programs in which proof of need was a basic requirement. As to the incidence of poverty, a better case
can be made for payments to families headed by women,
parents of minority groups, and unattached individuals than
for aged, farmers, veterans, and children in general. In
1968 about 22 percent of those persons over 64 living in
families were poor, 15 percent of all children were poor,
and 18 percent of all white farm residents were poor. Veterans receiving aid from programs which are primarily compensatory were probably not more than 15-20 percent poor.
But 35 percent of all families headed by women (58 percent
in the case of black families), 29 percent of all black families, 67 percent of all rural black families, 49 percent of
unrelated individuals over 64, and 29 percent of female unrelated individuals (18-64) were poor. [20]

Regardless of the implication of the above statistics,
it would be politically unwise and practically inefficient to
shift presumptive need to categories of greatest statistical
need. It might be better to forget the categorical system
entirely, or at least in the need-based programs, and institute the negative income tax principle to remove a poverty
income gap of twelve to fifteen billion dollars. This would
mean a return to emphasis on the demonstrated need principle, but an equitable and consistent means test would be
fairer, cheaper, and more adequate in the elimination of
substandard income than our present system of mixed categories.

Political Strategies for Poverty Elimination

The inadequacies of present public assistance and other income transfers as poverty elimination tools have been substantially documented. Persistent unemployment, inadequacies of the present welfare system, financial problems of state and local governments, alienation of disadvantaged groups, and priority shifts have brought proposals for welfare reform. The Mills-Nixon proposals offered floors under income of specified needy categories. The aged, blind and permanently disabled couple would receive $2,340 annually through the federal social security system, but the family assistance program would be much less adequate in relation to the $4,300 poverty line, for a family of no employment income would receive only $2,400. Families with a working member could receive up to $4,140 with payments being made through the federal Department of Health, Education and Welfare. Employables, including mothers of children six years of age and older (or three years of age and older after June 1974), would be expected to participate in manpower training programs and accept employment. In the face of persistent unemployment only $800 million for a projected 200,000 public service jobs is proposed. Consequently, opposition to the proposed legislation comes both from client and liberal power groups, who see inadequate income support for non-working families and inequities in forcing job training and employment acceptance, and from conservatives, who are concerned about costs and motivation toward leisure. The bill, HR1, passed with the family program excluded. Adult categories were placed under federal administration as of 1974 with minima of $130 for singles and $195 for couples.

Diverse groups might be united through a service income maintenance package which would benefit all. The key would be an access agency which would provide informational and referral services for all. Information would be provided on a variety of amenities and income support programs--everything from where to procure a dog license through how to get income support or psychiatric care. Such a system exists in Great Britain and there is a rapid growth of poorly supported informational and referral services in the United States and Canada. Federal aid should be provided to help citizens use our complex maze of social services. In addition, certain services now included largely under means test eligibility could be provided for all at no or minimal cost to the applicant. Examples are day care for children, child

growth and development programs, and services for the aged.
Rather generous legislation in these areas now has strong
support in Congress, but the legislation is not being related
to income maintenance programs as a package.

As to income maintenance, we would favor a limited,
equitable means test program rather than universal payments.
Universal payments which would provide a $4,300 family-of-
four income to all would cost over 225 billion dollars, or
over 100 billion dollars after tax recovery, while a means
test program, which would close the poverty gap, would cost
twelve-fifteen billion dollars above current welfare costs, or
twice those figures if a moderate work incentives provision
up to $6,000 annually for a family of four were to be in-
cluded.

Our contention is that a service trade-off for the
public, rather than expanding non-means test programs with
60-70 percent of the payments going to those above the current poverty line, would: (1) gain support of groups negative
to eliminating poverty; (2) provide better utilization of health,
education, and welfare systems; (3) act as an investment in
human resources which could prevent disorganization and enhance social and economic development; and (4) isolate
pathologies from income problems so that efficient restorative aid could be given in emotional and family relationship
problems with causes largely outside the income arena.
There are, currently, strong indications that tax reform
will have to precede welfare reform related to specific program changes.

The income maintenance-social utility package suggested above probably should be regarded as an interim step
toward the origination of a much more comprehensive health,
education and welfare master plan. We have abundant data
on needs and problems. We have much empirical evidence
of the failure of fragmented problems (e.g., the illiteracy
problem and plugging in a program to prevent school drop-
out). A systemic approach which considers the Gestalt of
problems is obviously needed.

A few years ago, the Department of Health, Education and Welfare was created to bring efficiency to the cha-
otic condition of the helping systems. So far, the results
are not encouraging. What we have is poorly coordinated
chaos. A master plan is needed both in the interest of efficiency and humanity.

Great Britain, a recognized leader in social welfare policy, effected coordination through the Beveridge Commission in the 1940s. Our President should appoint and our Congress should fund a study commission of an even broader scope. All of HEW coverage, plus such external problems as housing transportation and surplus food programs should be considered. The three principal charges should be:

1. The development of a comprehensive program in which consolidated and coordinated health, education and welfare programs support each other with specific legislative recommendations.
2. The origination of mechanisms for intervention in multi-problems areas--e.g. the central city ghetto.
3. A genuine redistributing income maintenance system.

Conclusions

We know the facts concerning the extent and incidence of poverty. There is still widespread public conviction that transfers to the poor, adequate enough to remove the poverty gap, would have a negative motivational effect and serve to impair economic progress, while grants to the more affluent would and do have only positive results. But the public is increasingly apt to challenge this double standard. The negative impact of inconsistent and punitive welfare policies is experiencing recognition, especially when it seems that these policies are costly and relatively non-effective in achieving program objectives. This discontent from new client power concentrations may soon be sufficient to produce change. A policy need is the development and acceptance of a new and consistent means test which will serve as a guide to an economical, but effective, welfare transfer payments system. The complexity and inharmonious condition of our present tax and welfare payments systems, as they relate to poverty, have exceeded the limits of public comprehension and acceptance. This confusion is, at least in part, the result of eighteenth century problems. It is time that we refocused on program simplicity, effectiveness in goal satisfaction, minimum cost, and maximum equity of tax-financed income maintenance programs. But much complexity in a complex world is inevitable, and universal access services coupled with limited income and service programs for special groups may bring adequate support for the poor, and positive results for our society.

Notes

1. See Blanche D. Coll, Perspective in Public Welfare
    (Washington, D. C. , U. S. Department of Health,
    Education and Welfare, 1969), pp. 1-7.

2. Vernon W. Ruttan, et al. , editors, Agricultural Policy
    in an Affluent Society (New York: W. W. Norton,
    1969) p. 132; or even more revealing is the fact that
    the top 137, 000 farmers, less than five percent of the
    total, received 46 percent of the $3. 7 billion made in
    1970 (See Helen Ginsburg, editor, Poverty, Eco-
    nomics and Society (Boston: Little, Brown and
    Company, 1972), p. 235.)

3. See Nick Kotz, Let Them Eat Promises: The Politics
    of Hunger in America (Englewood Cliffs: Prentice-
    Hall, Inc. , 1969).

4. Bertram Gross, "Friendly Fascism: A Model for
    America, " Social Policy, v. 1, no. 4, November-
    December, 1970, p. 48.

5. "Problem of Poverty in America, " Economic Report of
    the President, January, 1964, pp. 57-73.

6. Derived from data presented by Ida C. Merriam, Al-
    fred M. Skolnik, and Sophia R. Dales in "Social
    Welfare Expenditures, 1967-68, " Social Security
    Bulletin, v. 31, December, 1968, pp. 17-22.

7. Social Security Bulletin, v. 32, June, 1969, p. 47.

8. Ibid.

9. Based on estimate of 27 million in poverty. See Social
    Security Bulletin, v. 35 (November, 1972) p. 46.

10. Mollie Orshansky, "The Shape of Poverty in 1966, "
    Social Security Bulletin, v. 31, March, 1968, pp.
    28-29.

11. J. G. Turnbull, C. A. Williams, and B. F. Cheit,
    Economic and Social Security (New York: Ronald

Press, 1967), p. 105.

12.   See Dorothy K. Newman, "Changing Attitudes About the
      Poor," Monthly Labor Review, February, 1969, p.
      34.

13.   The near poor are hit harder than the very poor and
      middle income families, according to a 1960 based
      study by W. Irwin Gillespie which found tax incidence
      for families earning from $2,000 to $7,999 to be
      forty percent. See Alan B. Batchelder, The Eco-
      nomics of Poverty (New York: John Wiley, 1971),
      p. 168. "Income" does not include welfare trans-
      fers.

14.   See J. R. Pearman, A Survey of Income Maintenance
      Programs in Michigan (an unpublished dissertation,
      University of Minnesota, 1959), pp. 18-24, and
      Harry K. Girvetz, From Wealth to Welfare (Stan-
      ford, California: Stanford University Press, 1950),
      pp. 1-28 for elaboration of the motivational convic-
      tions of classical liberals.

15.   Edwin M. Lemert, Social Pathology (New York: Mc-
      Graw-Hill, 1951), p. 107.

16.   See Richard P. Applebaum, Theories of Social Change
      (Chicago: Markham Publishing Company, 1970), pp.
      65-99.

17.   See Raymond Mack, "The Components of Social Con-
      flict," in Ralph M. Kramer and Harry Specht, edi-
      tors, Readings in Community Organization Practice
      (Englewood Cliffs: Prentice-Hall, Inc., 1969), pp.
      327-330.

18.   See Warren C. Haggstrom, "Can the Poor transform
      the World?" Kramer and Specht, op. cit., pp. 301-
      314.

19.   William A. Gamson, Power and Discontent (Homewood,
      Illinois: The Dorsey Press, 1968), p. 189.

20.   Alan B. Batchelder, The Economics of Poverty, pp.
      21-25.

9. AGING IN AMERICA: GUIDELINES
   FOR ECONOMIC EDUCATION*

Preparation for aging is a lifetime process, although
the focus of education should respond to the interest and
motivation of the senior citizen at or near retirement. The
capacity of the older person to meet economic stress depends somewhat upon his accumulated knowledge and wealth
in addition to his current money income. The welfare of
the aged is also influenced by the degree of understanding
and sympathy of the public and the active involvement of the
senior citizen in efforts to improve his economic welfare.
Education in a variety of settings can greatly improve services and the use of services designed to promote the economic welfare of the aged.

Major objectives of diverse educational efforts include:

- To inform the public of economic problems concerning aging and to activate wide interest in voluntary and public
corrective policies which will better meet the needs of the
aged without destroying support for other vital programs,
e. g. , heavy community reliance on property tax may cause
school-millage-increase elections to fail as 80 percent of the
aged own homes and they face income pressure while getting
little direct service from the school system. The White
House Conference on Aging of 1961 provided much public
education which influenced policy, and the pending Second
White House Conference on Aging will provide incentive and
structure for citizen involvement on the local, state, and
national levels. Educational leaders should assume responsibility in this effort.

- To orient the young and middle-aged to the later
years, as well as to the other stages of the family life cycle, so that they may better plan their lives in relation to

*Reprinted from Social Education, Volume 35, Number 3,
March, 1971, with the permission of the publisher.

economic factors.   Much economic difficulty of the senior
citizen is caused by a lack of planning in the earlier years.

        - To directly provide economic education for the aged
so that they can make more effective use of their incomes
and savings; increase incomes through employment and en-
trepreneurship; become involved in seeking more effective
income maintenance programs while at the same time re-
specting the urgent needs of other economically deprived
groups.

Essential Economic Concepts Related to Objectives

        Aging brings conditions which intensify financial pres-
sures.   Our economy, which is based on a system of income
distribution roughly correlated with individual productivity,
builds in the forecast of declining incomes with advanced age
and the declining capacity to produce.   But old age is not
the only pressure point in the family cycle.   Of equal, if
not of greater current concern, is the disparate effort of individuals and beginning families with heads under 25 years
of age to meet their budgetary needs.   The right to earned
income value in our society threatens dependent persons of
all ages but especially so at both ends of the family life
cycle.   We are afraid that motivation will be destroyed by
transfer of small amounts of income from those who have
allegedly earned it to those who can not show a productive
effort for this income.

        Saving or private (including family) and public income
maintenance systems may compensate, in part, for the declining earning power of the aged, but several forces serve
to limit the effectiveness of these substitutes for adequate
wage and management incomes.   Those trying to teach or
learn remedies for the economic problems of aging need a
basic understanding of these limiting economic forces.

        The general conditions which serve to keep compen-
satory forces from making up deficits between budgetary
needs and productivity-induced income include:

        1.   The inability to accumulate sufficient savings and
the erosion of these limited savings and fixed incomes
through inflation.   The cost of living increased 30 percent
between 1960 and 1970, and the medical care component of
the cost of living increased 42 percent in the same period.[1]

Medical care costs were increasing twice as fast as the cost of living (all items) at the end of the decade.

2. A high and increasing dependency ratio (those below 21 and over 65 in relation to those 21 to 65) makes the family or taxpayer care-loads greater, and family capacity to help is not evenly distributed, i. e. , the lowest 20 percent of the family income groups receives about five percent of the total national income.

3. High interest rates erode income in the case of deferred payment and also tend to depress the value of the assets of the aged and others who might otherwise help them. Net returns divided by the rate of interest is a reflector of the value of real estate, stocks, and bonds. If the real or imputed net return on such assets remains unchanged and interest rates are doubled, property values are pushed toward a 50 percent decline in sale value, although speculation and rigidity in asset holding (even if a trade could be made for a more profitable investment) may prevent some of the decline.

4. We have heavy demands for governmental funds other than for the maintenance of adequate income for the young, the old, and the unfortunate. Approximately 50 percent of the federal budget goes for past and present military costs. All levels of government are concerned with pollution, slums, riots, and other environmental problems. Educational costs are large and increasing. There are many competing demands for the tax dollar.

Baseline Data on the Economics of Aging

The latest studies indicate that 30 percent of those over 65 are below the income-related poverty line ($3700 for an average family of four in mid-1970 or about $2500 for an aged couple). The aged poor make up 18 percent of the poverty group. But in comparison, 18. 5 percent of those under 18 are in poverty and they make up 43. 5 percent of the total poverty count. [2]

Budget-expenditure studies indicate problems for families headed by the young and the old which are of greater intensity than the budget problems of other families. Senate Committee hearings have provided data on the average position of families at various age intervals. Families with

heads under 25 have annual income deficits in relation to
expenditure varying from $67.00 for clerical to $1,384 for
self-employed. Of all major occupational categories, only
semi-skilled heads under 25 have a surplus of income over
expenditures. As families move through the life cycle to
the retirement period, appreciable surpluses occur in the
self-employed, professional, and skilled categories. But unskilled families have an average small surplus only in the
55-64 age span, and those families with clerical and semi-
skilled heads have small cumulative savings which fall short
of the income supplement need after age 65. [3]

    John R. Kerr, Associate Professor of Marketing at
Florida State University, has projected savings trends for
the young and aged families. He found a worsening of the
income-expenditure position of families with heads under 25
during the coming decade. He forecasted the following deficits by 1980: 12.2 percent for low income families, 3.9
percent for middle income families, and 7.9 percent for high
income families. The outlook for families with heads over
65 was found to be somewhat better than for the under-25-
age families. Disposable income for the aged group was
forecasted to grow faster than price increases, which, when
coupled with projected increases in Social Security retirement and Medicare benefits, was expected to result in the
aged families spending about 67 percent of their current income on current consumption as compared to 78 percent in
1965. [4] But persistent inflation has tended to erode projected
surpluses of all family age-level groupings.

    Despite projections which indicate more trouble for
young families and somewhat less trouble for families with
heads over 65, many aged have and will continue to have
major financial problems. Averages do not prove adequacy
for all. Savings are and will continue to be insufficient to
compensate for all inadequate incomes. According to a 1962
Social Security Administration estimate, median total asset
holdings of aged families was $5,840 with median liquid as-
sets of $570. [5] Most of these assets were in the home in-
habited by the family. Although two-thirds of the aged own
their own homes, 20 percent were mortgaged and 30 percent
were rated substandard.

    Relatively, families with heads over 65 do not fare
well as to income. Median income was 51 percent of that
of all younger families in 1961 as compared to 46 percent
in 1967. In this year, median income for families with a

head over 65 was $3,928 with about 20 percent of these families having incomes under $2000. Unattached individuals over 65 had a median income of $1480 with 25 percent receiving $1000 or less. Half of the senior citizen families have incomes below the Bureau of Labor Statistics moderate budget for a retired couple. One of the most pathetic conditions is that of the aged woman living alone. Seventy percent live in poverty.[6] It is clear that at least one-third of the 20 million persons aged 65 and older face severe economic challenges. Education can be an important tool in helping these individuals and families realize more from their restricted resources and in fostering public improvement of income maintenance programs.

Current Income Maintenance Program Weaknesses

There is little question as to the inadequacy of income maintenance and related supplementary service programs. The social security system has failed to keep pace with the rising cost of living and, in an even greater degree, with the income needs of the aged as described by the Bureau of Labor Statistics Moderate Standard of Living for Retired Couples (approximately $4500 in mid-1970). Average figures on payments to the aged through the major income maintenance programs were: Old Age Assistance, $74.95 per month, and the Old Age, Survivors and Disability Insurance basic benefit, $100.76 per month. As of December 31, 1968, the average OASDI benefit per family was $100.90 per month.[7] Medicare met only 35 percent of all health costs of the aged during the year 1967. The health cost average was $486 or 2 3/4 times the average cost for younger persons in 1967.[8]

The Special Senate Committee on Aging has singled out five problems of the aging which need immediate attention. These pressing needs are:

- Income supplementation for widows who constitute the most disadvantaged group.
- The problem of meeting health needs in the face of rapidly rising medical costs.
- Problems related to home ownership, home maintenance, and taxation. (Especially the heavy reliance on property taxes for state and local revenue.)
- Improvement of employment opportunities for the aged.

Implications of early retirement trends. (This
would include such considerations as increased
problems of income maintenance, loss of the productive efforts of the aged, and emotional and social impacts.)[9]

Our public income maintenance effort for the aged is
not impressive in light of our high productivity when compared with other countries. We spend about 7.6 of national
consumption expenditures for all welfare benefits as contrasted with 8.3 in Japan, 12.4 in Canada, 13.5 in the United
Kingdom, 18.6 in France, 20.8 in Austria, and 21 percent
in West Germany.[10] We need to carefully consider revision
of our income maintenance program in light of our affluence,
but there are other approaches which may also serve to lift
the living level of our senior citizens.

Educational Solutions

There are avenues for education in a variety of agencies at all stages of the family life cycle, i.e., premarital
youth, the beginning family, the growing family, the con-
tracting family, the retired couple, and single consumers.
Education is a function of many social institutions and social
organizations--the formal educational system, religion, social welfare agencies, business, libraries, museums, etc.--
and all may contribute something constructive toward education for the aging. I will not attempt to discuss the contributions of each but rather to outline some general areas in
which an informed and talented educational effort may provide constructive results. Goals should be specific and out-
comes should be measured, in so far as possible, in terms
of input-output relationships.

1. Educators have an important role in informing the
public as to the inadequacies of our income maintenance system in relation to our potential to help. The effort should
be factually informative, and alternative solutions should be
presented, rather than being propagandistic in a biased and
indoctrinating sense. Some of the pertinent facts are presented in this article. Much other related material is available through the findings of the United States Senate Special
Committee on Aging and through a large library offering of
research and other written materials on the economic problems of aging. Several specific goals may be set by educators. I will not try to list them all, but certainly one of

the primary goals should be that of developing the concept that economic disaster is not a logical expectation because of our current welfare effort for the aged and other needy persons.

2.   Our income maintenance and service system is very complex.   Well-informed social brokers in various health and welfare agencies can perform a valuable educational service in connecting aged persons with the most effective public and private services at minimum costs in money and frustration.   For example, the Florida Division of Family and Children's Services began the fiscal year 1971 by appointing 47 "ombudsmen" to act in liaison between aged clients and the services which they need.   The advocate in relation to the establishment, which is the Scandinavian function for an ombudsman, was not included but his is also an important liaison function.   In addition to the brokerage function, the education of paraprofessional and indigenous personnel by welfare supervisors or through special school-based educational programs is important to the welfare of the needy aged.   In order to fulfill the roles mentioned above, teachers and supervisors must know very well all social systems, e.g., economic, educational, welfare, health, including the detailed knowledge of programs which have been especially designed to meet the needs of the aged.

3.   Special adult education directed at the aged in general or their indigenous leaders has much potential for assisting the aging with economic problems.   As an example, Project Moneywise was directed toward helping the aged handle their financial problems more intelligently.   The project was sponsored by the Bureau of Federal Credit Unions and funded through the Office of Economic Opportunity.   A four-week consumer education program covering the following areas was offered:

a.   An overview of the general consumer education problem.
b.   Consumer education in relation to special problems of the elderly.
c.   Marketing education related to the exploitation of the aged through high pressure peddlers, mail order fraud, weak consumption patterns, and general marketing knowledge failure.
d.   How to recognize and handle fraudulent and deceptive sales practices.
e.   Financial and budgeting skills for the elderly.

f. Credit costs and how to use credit wisely.
g. Discussion of available community services re-
    lated to consumer problems.
h. Information as to federal programs which provide
    aid to aged persons, e. g., Social Security, Medi-
    care and Medicaid, Quackery and Fraud Control,
    Drug Control, Public Health Services, and Hous-
    ing.
i. Development of the aged consumer's understand-
    ing of consumer cooperatives and credit unions
    as substitute for high cost retailing and loan
    agencies.
j. The principles of leadership and community or-
    ganization practice. [11]

4. Course content on the economics of aging and the
solutions to problems can logically be included in high school
social studies classes. As with any attempt at the application of economics principles, the instructor should have at
least a minimum of formal education in the subject. We
have been making some progress in the economics preparation of social studies teachers, but in 1961, 77 percent of
our social studies teachers did not meet the Committee on
Economic Development minimum standard of six semester
hours. [12] Those instructors lacking minimal course work in
economics should move to erase this deficiency. Instruction
on the problems of aging should treat the whole person; the
student should be helped to conceptualize the gestalt of aging, but that which is economics should be recognized and
correctly presented.

I shall not present a detailed unit on economic education for aging, but rather furnish some guidelines for presenting the course content.

- In line with the concept of beginning at or near
  where the student is, it might be helpful to preface
  the course content on the aged with a review of the
  economic problems of the young, newly-married
  couple where the income-expenditure gap is known
  to be great. Facts can be presented, reasons for
  the problem can be explored, personal planning
  solutions derived, and ameliorating governmental
  action, e. g. tax policy impact or finance of post-
  high school education, recommended. Significant
  economic concepts can be taught within this problems frame. For example, Paul Samuelson, the

eminent economist from Massachusetts Institute of
Technology, recently received wide publicity for his
remark that there was only one thing worse than an
income-restricting approach to controlling inflation
which doesn't work and that is one that does achieve
this purpose. His reference is to restrictive fiscal
and monetary policies which control money supply
(holding the growth of money to four percent) and
strive to control purchasing power by curtailing
employment and governmental aid to the least fortunate and most vulnerable elements in our society.
An implication is that the induced unemployment
will fall most heavily upon youth, aged, minority
groups, poorly trained, and those employed on government projects which are being curtailed as a
part of fiscal policy. A further result is that price
decline is the greatest for entrepreneurs who are
highly competitive, such as farmers and most small
retailers. Also, consistency in the current inflation
control policy would limit spending for education
and welfare. And so, while it is true that inflation
hurts those aged with fixed incomes, income-related monetary and fiscal control policies hurt the
aged person's chances for employment and more
adequate welfare payments. The young and the old
have a common ground for suffering the consequences of inadequate income.

- In the interest of brevity, it seems non-essential
  to recount the exact content of a unit on economic
  problems in aging. The income and consumption
  problems of the aged have been specifically high-
  lighted earlier in this paper and outlines can be
  drawn up from this content.

- The high school student, who has been challenged
  by the introduction of economic problems which
  will face him now or in the near future, should
  carry some motivation over to the problems of the
  later years. But further motivational efforts may
  be necessary. Role playing, emulation, and games
  which provide upsets in well-made retirement
  plans, such as inflation, depression, and automation, might be used to lead into important economic
  concepts on how to hedge or insure against such
  catastrophes.

Projects which would provide a coordinated frame
for student efforts promise additional learning
gains. A logical current project might be the
equivalent of adult preparation for the White House
Conference on Aging with class recommendations
being forwarded to the local delegates to that pending conference. Resource persons from the state
office on aging, the old age assistance program,
the social security office, and stock brokerage
firms, among others, might be utilized.

We need to approach the problems of aging at all age
levels to insure the best problem-preventive gains, and the
high school social studies class provides an important opportunity to achieve this objective. Students may be helped to
recognize a commonality of problems of old and young, to
realize the universality of basic economic concepts, and to
better understand the special problems of aging. We should
also exert more educational effort to helping the aged directly or in improving the capacity of agents who are supposed to be helping them.

Notes

1.   Federal Reserve Bulletin (June, 1970), v. 56, no. 6,
         Table 66.

2.   Sar A. Levitan, Programs in Aid of the Poor for the
         1970's. Baltimore: Johns Hopkins Press, 1969,
         p. 5.

3.   Economics of Aging: Toward a Full Share of Abun-
         dance. Hearings before the Special Committee on
         Aging, U. S. Senate, 91st Congress, First Session,
         1969, Part I, p. 217.

4.   John R. Kerr, "An Expanding Market for Installment
         Credit" (mimeographed) and "Income and Expendi-
         tures: The Over-65 Age Group, " Journal of Geron-
         tology (January, 1968), 23, pp. 78-81.

5.   Economics of Aging: Toward a Full Share of Abun-
         dance, op. cit. , Part I, p. 194.

6.   Ibid. , pp. 155-189.

7.   Social Security Bulletin, June, 1970.

8.   Economics of Aging: Toward a Full Share of Abun-
       dance, op. cit., Part I, p. 171.

9.   Ibid., Part I, p. 158.

10.   Ibid., Part I, p. 74.

11.   Economics of Aging: Toward a Full Share of Abun-
       dance, op. cit., Part II, p. 417.

12.   See Research and Policy Committee for Economic De-
       velopment, Economic Literacy for Americans.   New
       York: Committee for Economic Development, 1962,
       p. 13.

10. EQUITY AND INEQUITY IN OUR LEGAL SYSTEM*

Individual welfare is determined, in part, by the relative power of individuals and groups as they stand before decision-making governmental tribunals. This statement is made despite the obvious "talking power" of money, as government is frequently the final arbiter as to income and social utility or amenity distribution. Wide differentials are due both to acts of commission and omission before the law. Legislative, executive and judicial decisions may be directed negatively or positively toward specific classes or groups despite the equality pronouncement of the Great American Creed.

The term "law" need not refer solely to statutes of the criminal code or requirements of eligibility for aid passed by the Congress and state legislatures; the term may also be used in reference to the administrative regulations that permeate the welfare field and to the procedural rules that control access to the courts. Although many of these administrative and procedural rules are not "laws" in the statutory sense of the term, they affect people in the same way and are often just as binding. For instance, a common regulation that must be agreed upon in many states in order to receive Aid to Families of Dependent Children is to allow field investigations by welfare workers at any time during the working day. Whether or not the field "visit" regulation is in the state statutes, it has a very real and concrete impact on AFDC recipients, and to them it is a "law."

The United States Supreme Court and some of the state courts have in recent years shown an increasing awareness of the peculiar problems facing the indigent caught up in our legal processes. There remains much to be done by individuals in the helping professions to effect further change.

*Published with the permission of the principal co-author Edward L. Harvey, BSW, and senior law school student at Florida State University.

It is a common contention that many of our society's laws and the procedures involved in enforcing them discriminate adversely against people of low socio-economic status. Some are written intentionally to affect only those people falling into certain categories, such as those dealing with deception and fraud in welfare applications; they apply to welfare recipients but not to the general population as do the regulations dealing with "errors" on income tax forms. Some of the laws, such as those pertaining to juvenile delinquency or bail, were intended to affect all classes impartially, but as a result of several interrelated and unanticipated factors they often tend to weigh most heavily against the poor and the ethnic minorities. Finally, whether or not the law was intended to affect the poor to a greater or lesser degree than the general population, many laws have unanticipated, long-range adverse effects which are not discovered until the poor have already borne their burden too long to easily forget. There is as much justification for a more systemic approach to the law enforcement and judicial systems as for other social systems. Planning in the face of social change and the utilization of feedback to assist in the amendment of laws and procedures is crucial to more effective safety and equity goals.

This chapter attempts to bring some illustrative problems into clear focus and suggest some methods by which existing inequities are being or could be removed from our legal system.

Unequal Effects of the Application and Enforcement of the Criminal Code upon the Poor

The Juvenile Justice System

In the area of juvenile delinquency we find a wide variety of definitions of "delinquent" or "criminal" as they refer to the behavior of minors. The first juvenile court in the United States was established in Cook County, Illinois, in 1899. The Illinois statute that established the court defined delinquency essentially as a form of "child crime," that is, any act which if committed by an adult would be considered a crime.[1] Since the Illinois juvenile court was founded, however, the laws defining delinquency in the various states have developed in very broad and inconsistent

directions. While some states remain close to the doctrine
of "child crime," others have gone far beyond this limitation; they may also cover various prohibitions against "child
immorality," such as incorrigibility, habitual truancy, en-
dangering one's health and morals, and other forms of behavior that are not considered illegal when engaged in by
adults.[2] There are a number of states which do not define
delinquency in their statutes at all. In these states, say
Martin and Fitzpatrick in their discussion of the subject,
"...delinquency is whatever the particular court hearing a
case says it is."[3]

     The lack of exact definitions of delinquency leaves the
juvenile in a rather unique position. On one hand, if he has
committed a "child crime" but is remanded to a juvenile
court, he has the advantage of not being subject to the adult
criminal justice system with its criminal courts and correc-
tional institutions. On the other hand, a juvenile who is
adjudged "delinquent" for behavior that would not be considered criminal were he an adult is faced with quite another
situation. He may be placed in a "training school" until
the age of twenty-one, an obvious disadvantage when compared
to an adult engaged in performing the same behavior.

     Until very recently the major criticism leveled at ju-
venile courts was the informality of their procedures and the
total disregard for the rights of the juveniles involved. In
fact the Supreme Court held in the case In re Holmes in
1955 that juvenile courts were not required to extend the
constitutional rights accorded to adults to the juveniles involved in their proceedings.[4] However, the Supreme Court
of 1967 held in the Gault case that "...juveniles are entitled
to formal notice of the charges against them, the right of
legal counsel, the right of confrontation and cross-examina-
tion of witnesses, the privilege of protection against self-
incrimination, the right to a transcript of proceedings, and
the right to appeal."[5]

     Since the decision in Gault there has been some con-
fusion among the lower courts as to the actual scope to be
accorded the pronouncement in that case. The Court had
clearly accorded juvenile offenders additional due process
protection, but no one knew how much. For instance, was
the juvenile court still to be considered closer to a "civil"
tribunal rather than a "criminal" court?

     In 1970, the Court seemed to answer the question

when it handed down its decision in In re Winship 397 U. S.
358 (1970).   The case involved the burden of proof to be
required when convicting a juvenile of an act which would be
considered criminal if done by an adult.   Section 744 (b) of
the New York Family Court Act required only proof "on the
preponderance of the evidence" in juvenile court proceedings.
The Defendant's claim that the Fourteenth Amendment required proof "beyond a reasonable doubt" of every fact necessary to constitute the crime alleged was upheld by the
Supreme Court on the basis of the Due Process Clause.

     The last two cases reported on the subject of due
process as it affects the juvenile were handled down by the
Court in a consolidated opinion: McKiever v. Pennsylvania
and In re Burrus 91 S. Ct. 1976 (1971).   In both of these
cases the defendants were charged with acts which would
have been considered "criminal" if done by an adult, and
they both faced possible confinement until they reached their
majority.   The Court, in an opinion announced by Mr. Justice Blackmun, held that due process did not entitle the defendants to a jury trial in the adjudicative phase of a state
juvenile court delinquency proceeding.   The decision was
based upon the fact that the Sixth Amendment entitled persons to an impartial jury "in all criminal prosecutions. "
The juvenile court proceeding is not a "criminal prosecution"
within the meaning of the Sixth Amendment, stated the Court,
and therefore the applicable standard was "fundamental fair-
ness" with an emphasis on fact finding procedures, as developed in Gault and Winship.   The Court then stated: "But
one cannot say that in our legal system the jury is a necessary component of accurate fact finding. "

     The decision was rendered over a strongly worded
dissent by Justices Douglas, Black, and Marshall.   They
read Gault to say that "neither the Fourteenth Amendment
nor the Bill of Rights is for adults alone, " and continued
with an in-depth criticism of the manner in which juvenile
cases were handled by the States.   The dissenting justices
felt that since each defendant faced a possible five-year sentence, and one could have received a ten-year sentence,
they were entitled to jury trials; "... no adult could be denied
a jury trial in those circumstances. "   It was felt that trial
by jury would provide a safeguard against "being pre-judged
by a judge who may well be prejudiced by reports already
submitted to him by the police or caseworkers in the case. "

     The statutes and rulings regarding what constitutes

delinquent behavior have a clear potential to discriminate adversely against juveniles. The informality of the juvenile justice system was conceived of as a method of relieving the youthful offender of some of the harshness of the adult system. Although born of an attitude of benevolence, this very informality has resulted in the abuses that are most frequently criticized today.

In Gibbons' discussion of differential treatment of youths who come in contact with police, he cites a number of studies which seem to indicate that the socio-economic class of the youth does not have a significant impact on the treatment of the case, at least as in regard to the more serious offenses.[6] He does go on, however, to mention a number of rather subtle factors which may enter into the picture. Aside from serious offenses, which most police handle routinely in a strict legalistic manner, Gibbons cites "personal characteristics" of the youths to be the main determinants of police action.[7] Among the most important are the youth's attitude toward the officer and his "general demeanor." Much of the hostile reaction on the part of the youths, especially lower class residents of ghettos, comes as a result of the high level of police attention and harassment given to these areas of our larger cities.[8] The constant surveillance and harassment may lead to the hostile reactions, which in turn leads to high rates of referral to juvenile courts for relatively minor offenses among ghetto youths.

Once a youth gets referred to the court his case is again subject to a great deal of discretion on the part of officials, especially intake officers and judges, both of whom can decide to dismiss the juvenile or pursue the case further. In summarizing a number of studies which deal with factors involved in the disposition of juvenile cases, Gibbons states that the problem is very complex and that there is too little factual data available to generalize as to the effect of poverty or ethnic background on the dispositions. He does state, however, that poverty and minority class status may indirectly influence the adjudication and sentencing of youthful offenders, especially in larger communities and in departments which employ probation officers who are subject to strong community pressures for punitive treatment.[9] Martin and Fitzpatrick, in their discussion of the influence of social class upon apparently higher rates of delinquency and more the severe treatment of adjudicated offenders, cite two major forces as being at least partly responsible:

"... the relative inability of the poor to purchase help ...
and the relatively few opportunities afforded the poor to en-
gage in 'safe' forms of deviation ... 'white collar' crime
... as opposed to 'common law' crimes such as robbery and
assault which are more rigorously prosecuted."[10]

In summary, the juvenile justice system consists of
a vague set of statutes and regulations defining delinquent
behavior and an enforcement procedure which allows a high
degree of discretion as to the handling and disposition of
cases on the part of the police, the probation "intake" officers, and the judges themselves. The vagueness of the
laws, and the discretionary power of the officers, tend to
create a situation which is at least potentially open to discriminatory application of sanctions toward the lower socio-
economic classes and ethnic minority groups. Whether or
not discrimination actually takes place is unclear from available data at the present time; however, some studies cited
above do indicate a higher arrest and referral rate for
youths of low socioeconomic status and minority group membership. This correlation is also brought out in the length
and severity of sentences. The variables involved are complex, however, and it is difficult to pinpoint any one factor
as the main reason for the differences. It is enough to say
that there is some indication that lower class youths, especially in ghettos, seem to be affected more severely than
middle class or upper class white youths by the juvenile
justice system. Social workers who are serving in broker
or advocate roles for delinquent youth must learn the particular attributes of the courts which have jurisdiction over
their clients; and they must develop the skills needed to
operate effectively within this "quasi-judicial" system.

Bail Practices

The poor are adversely affected by our present system of bail in a number of important ways. The purpose
of bail is essentially to assure the accused's presence at
the trial. Traditionally, heavy reliance is placed on financial risk as an incentive for the accused to appear in court.
Bail is theoretically used as a vehicle to allow accused offenders their freedom to prepare adequate defense based on
the presupposition of innocence. It is also used to keep the
already overcrowded jails and detention facilities from becoming completely unmanageable. The eighth amendment to
the Constitution prohibits "excessive bail," but does not, in

terms, confer an absolute right to bail. Rule 46 of the
Federal Rules of Criminal Procedure does explicitly state
the right to bail:

> (a) Right to Bail. (1) Before conviction. A per-
> son arrested for an offense not punishable by death
> shall be admitted to bail. A person arrested for
> an offense punishable by death may be admitted to
> bail by any court or Judge authorized by law to do
> so in the exercise of discretion, giving due weight
> to the evidence and to the nature and circum-
> stances of the offense. [11]

Aside from the weight of evidence and the nature and circumstances of the crime, courts also are supposed to consider the amount necessary to reasonably assure the defendant's appearance, the financial condition of the accused, and
the defendant's character when determining bail. [12]

In the actual performance of the bail system, however, we find that it fails to perform its function in a number of important ways. Frequently a bail-bondsman actually
determines whether or not the defendant is released. Also,
judges use high bail determination as "punishment" for defendants or in an attempt to break "crime waves." Of the
many factors which judges take into consideration, perhaps
the least important to them is the relationship between the
amount of bail and the defendant's financial status. In their
discussion of the bail system Ares, Rankin, and Sturz state
that, "Perhaps the most serious indictment of the bail system is that it discriminates against the poor."[13] They compare detention before trial to "punishment of a person not
convicted of a crime." In their study of the effect of detention upon case dispositions Ares, Rankin, and Sturz reveal statistics which clearly show the adverse effects upon
persons not able to make bail. They found that persons
not incarcerated at the time of trial stood a better chance
of receiving a favorable disposition of their cases. They
also found differences in the length of sentences given to
persons in detention as opposed to persons out on bail, with
significantly longer sentences given to those persons in cus-
tody and found guilty of the charges of assault in the third
degree, possession of dangerous weapons, and petit and
grand larceny, all crimes which are common to the lower
socio-economic classes. [14]

The discrimination perpetrated against the poor may

be unintended, but nevertheless it is very real in its effect
and very unjust in its results.   The widespread use of set
bail schedules, keyed to the charge rather than the man,
restricts the flexibility which is the basis of bail.   The effects upon the economically deprived defendant are a viable
indictment against the bail system as practiced presently in
our courts.

The Supreme Court of Florida has recently made extensive revisions in the Florida Rules of Criminal Procedure
which promise to alleviate many of the current inequities of
the bail system.   The rules, approved October 16, 1972,
have the effect of law under the Florida Constitution, which
gives the Supreme Court exclusive jurisdiction under which
to proclaim rules governing the procedures to be followed in
that state's courts.   Under Rule 3.130 of the Florida Rules
of Criminal Procedure the committing magistrate now has
the discretion to release the defendant on his own recognizance in all cases except the few considered "non-bailable. "
The rules were changed for the express purpose of lessening
the influence of bail bondsmen on the bail process.   Judges
are instructed that since the purpose of bail is to "insure
the defendant's appearance, " the judge shall consider "all the
relevant factors to determine whether bail is necessary";
and if bail is not considered necessary to assure the defendant's appearance the judge may "in his discretion, release
a defendant on his own recognizance. " The ultimate effect
of the change is, at this writing, uncertain.   Florida Supreme
Court Justice Richard Irwin, dissenting to the new rule,
thought that the court did not go far enough.   He felt that
the power of the trial judge should have been further restricted and that most defendants should be released without
bond upon their promise to appear in court, in order to
eliminate "one more means of discriminating against the
poor. "

Legal Counsel and the Poor

The importance of legal counsel in a court of law is
largely unquestioned.   Whether the indigent person is involved in a civil suit or a criminal action the presence of a
lawyer to act in his behalf is almost a necessity if he hopes
to be successful.

The importance of legal counsel to persons charged
with a felony was recognized by the Supreme Court in 1963

when, in Gideon v. Wainwright,[15] the court held that in
cases involving the possibility of long sentences a defendant
has a fundamental right to legal counsel, whether or not he
is financially able to furnish it personally.

In 1972, the Supreme Court held in Argersinger v.
Hamlin -U. S. -, 32 L. Ed. 2d 530 (1972) that a defendant is
entitled to counsel whenever he faces possible incarceration
under a relevant state statute for any length of time. This
decision, a substantial broadening of the Gideon decision,
will no doubt aid indigent defendants, who up until now were
not entitled to state-provided counsel unless facing possible
incarceration for a period of six months or greater.

Under the new Florida Rules of Criminal Procedure,
Rule 3.111, entitled "Providing Counsel for the Indigent, "
the Florida Supreme Court has again attempted to erase certain inequities existing under the former system. The rule
provides for appointment of counsel when the defendant is
formally charged, or as soon as feasible after custodial re-
straint, or upon his first appearance before a committing
magistrate, whichever occurs earliest.

Counsel is provided to any indigent or "partially-in-
digent" person charged with an offense which may result in
imprisonment or incarceration in a juvenile corrections institution, including appeals from convictions thereof. The
only exception is when a judge files a statement in writing
that the defendant to a misdemeanor or municipal ordinance
charge will not be imprisoned in the event he is convicted.

The addition of the "partially indigent" category is
aimed at alleviating the tremendous costs of preparing an
adequate defense by persons "unable to pay more than a
portion of the fee charged by an attorney, including costs of
investigation, without substantial hardship to himself or his
family. " Such a person need only request a state-appointed
counsel and promise to defray a portion of the expenses according to his ability. This category should provide relief
to a great many clients who would not be able to qualify as
totally indigent, but who nevertheless would be unable to retain a private counsel and undertake the costs of investigation necessary to prepare an adequate defense.

The importance of receiving legal counsel is not con-
fined merely to a court of law. Increasingly, it has become
apparent that the pre-trial and "custodial" stages of a

criminal case require protection for the accused offenders involved. In 1966 the Supreme Court held, in Miranda v. Arizona, [16] that a suspect must be informed of his rights to remain silent, and to the services of legal counsel, at no cost if he is indigent, before any interrogation takes place. These rights must be presented to the suspect clearly and all questioning must cease once he advises the police that he wishes to remain silent or wants legal assistance. [17] These cases have been important in establishing the right to legal counsel for the indigent and have marked the realization that the presence of counsel is important in all stages of the criminal justice system.

The poor also need the assistance of legal counsel in civil and administrative actions in which they may be involved for the protection of their rights in such areas as consumer affairs, landlord difficulties, and infringements upon privacy. Most communities have Legal Aid Societies, composed of local bar members, which try to meet these particular needs of the poor. In a talk given on the Florida State University campus, [18] Robert McLure described the functions of the Tallahassee Legal Aid Society. As an example of limited service, the Legal Aid Society in Tallahassee was not affiliated with any other organizations and it only handled civil suits. It was available on a five-day-a-week basis to any "bonafide or borderline indigent with a bonafide legal problem." The determination of indigence was left up to the lawyer on duty that day, but the service given was free and reputed to be equal to that given paying clients. The Society also used several Florida State University Law School students as research assistants as a result of a Florida Supreme Court ruling that third year law school students may under supervision argue cases in court for indigent parties. Some legal aid programs, especially those sponsored by the Office of Economic Opportunity, employ full-time staff and comprehensive services are provided with a strong advocacy commitment for the poor who come before the courts.

Legal services for the poor are also being assisted by several technical and research programs (16 were listed in the July, 1972 issue of the Clearinghouse Review) in several of our larger cities. Two of the more comprehensive programs which have been most helpful to instructors and students have been the National Clearing House for Legal Services at Northwestern University, which publishes the Clearinghouse Review, and the Project on Social Welfare Law which was conducted under a grant by the New York University Law School. One report of the Project dealt extensively with the problems of low income consumers.[19]

Due Process, Equal Protection and the Supreme Court

The United States Supreme Court decisions have established two bases upon which the Court has been willing to rely in protecting the rights and equalizing the treatment of indigent persons. The basis being advanced in a number of recent cases is the Equal Protection Clause of the Fourteenth Amendment. The Due Process Clause, which is the more traditional approach, is relied on as the main basis by the majority of the Justices in their written opinions; and it seems to be more easily accepted, less "radical" in image, than the Equal Protection rationale.

In Tate v. Short, 401 U. S. 395 (1971), the Court considered the effect of a Texas law requiring that persons unable to pay monetary fines resulting from traffice offenses be incarcerated a sufficient time to satisfy their fines at the rate of $5.00 per day. Defendant had accumulated $425.00 in fines on nine traffice offenses, requiring an 85-day term of confinement. Persons able to pay could not be imprisoned under the statute. The Court held that the Equal Protection Clause requires that the statutory ceiling placed on imprisonment for any substantive offense be the same for all defendants irrespective of their economic status. Since Texas had legislated a "fines only" policy, the statutory ceiling could not be converted to a prison term for an indigent person without means to pay.

In Boddie v. Connecticut, 401 U. S. 371 (1971), welfare recipients challenged certain State procedures as restricting their access to the courts in bringing an action for divorce. The procedures in question, requiring court fees and costs for service of process amounting to an average of $60.00 which the petitioners were unable to pay, were struck down by the Court as they affected indigent persons under two theories. Justices Douglas and Brennan filed concurring opinions based upon the Equal Protection Clause. Justice Harlan, speaking for the Court, struck down the procedures on a Due Process rationale, stating, "...persons forced to settle their claims of right and duty through the judicial process must be given a meaningful opportunity to be heard."

The Court's decisions have not all been promising.
As mentioned above, there seems to be developing a basis
upon which to argue that discrimination based upon indigency
is proscribed by the Equal Protection Clause just as is discrimination based upon race.   This may seem elementary,
but the Supreme Court has been reluctant through the years
to use that clause to strike down State action which was
discriminatory, unless there was a clear showing of radical
discrimination.

In 1971 the Supreme Court handed down its decision
in James v. Valtierra, 402 U.S. 137 (1971), involving a
California amendment to the State Constitution, Article
XXXIV, providing that no low rent housing project could be
"developed, constructed, or acquired in any manner by a
state public body until the project was approved by a majority of those voting at a community election. " The suit was
brought by citizens eligible for low cost housing in a community where officials could not apply for available federal
funds because low-cost housing proposals had been defeated
in local referendums.   A three-judge federal court held the
Article in question unconstitutional as denying the plaintiffs
equal protection.   The court relied on a 1969 case involving
an Akron, Ohio referendum provision struck down in Hunter
v. Erickson, 393 U.S. 385 (1969).   The Supreme Court, in
overruling the lower court, distinguished Hunter on the
ground that the Akron referendum was held to be discriminatory on "distinctions based on race, " while Article XXXIV
"requires referendum approval for any low-rent housing project, not only for projects which will be occupied by a racial minority. " Great emphasis was placed on California's
"long history of allowing voter referenda on matters of community and statewide interest. "

The plaintiffs had also pointed to California's history
of allowing local referenda on matters of local interest.
They drew a distinction, which was rejected by the Supreme
Court, between allowing voters on their own initiative the
privilege of rejecting local programs that had been put into
effect and that would increase their taxes; and imposing a
mandatory vote requirement on one type of program, to take
place before any action could be taken on its implementation.
Since all other projects, including housing projects, were
subject to the former procedure, it was felt that imposing
the latter referendum on low-income housing projects only
was an inherently discriminatory burden placed on the plaintiffs because of their indigence.

The dissenting opinion, filed by Mr. Justice Marshall and joined by Justices Brennan and Blackmun, strongly disputed both the reasoning and the basis of the majority's opinion. They pointed out that publicly-assisted housing developments designed to accommodate the aged, veterans, state employees, persons of moderate income, or ". . . any class of citizens other than the poor, need not be approved by prior referanda. " Article XXXIV was by its very terms an explicit classification on the basis of poverty--"suspect classification which demands exacting judicial scrutiny. " Justice Marshall, in closing his dissent, stated what some thought had been already established as the philosophy of the Equal Protection Clause: ". . . It is far too late in the day to contend that the Fourteenth Amendment prohibits only racial discrimination; and to me, singling out the poor to bear a burden not placed on any other class of citizens tramples the values that the Fourteenth Amendment was designed to protect. "

Other recent decisions by the Supreme Court have upheld principles of equity and due process in such areas as the right to a fair hearing prior to grant reductions or suspensions (Goldberg v. Kelley),[20] the right of AFDC payments for children whose father is absent from the home because of military service (Carleson v. Remillard, 92 S. Ct. 1932, 40 LW 4624 [1972]),[21] and the right of aliens to welfare payments (Graham v. Richardson, 403 U. S. 365 [1971]).[22] The trend may be in the direction of greater equity for welfare clients but the process is slow. Social workers must be continually and primarily educated to perform the social brokerage function so that welfare clients may gain access to rightful benefits under the welfare system; since legislative, executive and judicial changes do not automatically guarantee additional help for clients.

Conclusions

In her article, "Poverty and Criminal Justice, " which was presented to the President's Commission on Law Enforcement and Administration of Justice, Patricia Wald discussed the plight of the poor persons as he is swept along through the machinery of our criminal justice system. She summarizes,

> Poverty breeds crime. The poor are arrested more often, convicted more frequently, sentenced

> more harshly, rehabilitated less successfully than
> the rest of society. So long as the social condi-
> tions which produce poverty remain, no reforms
> in the criminal process will eliminate this imbal-
> ance. But we can ease the burdens of poverty by
> assuring the poor those basic procedural rights
> which our society ostensibly grants all citizens:
> the right to be represented by competent counsel
> early enough in the process to preserve other
> rights; the right to prepare an adequate defense,
> the right to be free until convicted, the right not
> to be jailed solely because of lack of money to re-
> mit a fine or make restitution, the right to parole,
> the right to make a clean start after prison. In
> withholding these fundamental rights from any citi-
> zens, society reveals a poverty of its own. [23]

Several imperfections in our legal system deter equity
for the poor, but this does not eliminate an important role
for social workers and other similar helping service personnel. The worker who knows legal systems, functional procedures, and legal aid resources can help the client to obtain
much needed help. This service, and a constructive approach toward mobilizing for needed structural changes in
the system, are important roles for helping service personnel with an interest in seeing their clients obtain justice and
equity under our legal system.

The Use of Welfare Regulations as a Means of Control
Over the Personal Behavior of the Poor

Social Control

We have seen how laws and legal procedures sometimes affect the poor differently than members of other por-
tions of our society. For the most part differences in treatment are probably unintended, and are due to unknown factors
influencing arrest rates, disposition of cases, and sentencing
procedures in the criminal justice system.

There is a basic difference of opinion as to what the
criteria should be when evaluating an application for aid.
The belief that aid should be based on need alone is professed by most professional workers in the welfare field.

This belief enjoys its greatest level of acceptance from the general public in cases of the physically handicapped, cases which involve "involuntary dependency. "

    We do not find the same acceptance in the Aid to Dependent Children programs. In his chapter entitled "The Politics of Eligibility, "[24] Steiner brought out a number of reasons why he thinks eligibility based on need alone is not widely accepted today in regard to AFDC programs. When AFDC programs were first begun, asserted Steiner, the major reason for children's dependency was the death of the father; of all AFDC cases in 1937, 88% were due to this factor. That percentage had dropped to less tha 7% in 1962, with desertion and unwed pregnancies now constituting the major reasons for dependency. [25] This switch from "involuntary dependency" to what is considered "voluntary dependency" has resulted in a hardening of public attitude toward AFDC cases and increased demand for methods to make sure recipients are "worthy" of aid. Public concern has grown as the number of AFDC recipients (over 10 million) has doubled in ten years.

    In order to receive aid, therefore, a person applying for AFDC today must not only be in need, but must be "worthy, " demonstrating worthiness by making certain sacrifices. The work test is being revived and AFDC mothers usually have to consent to invasions of their privacy by being subject to welfare searches; they are pushed toward low paying jobs or job training for non-existent jobs; and they must structure their personal lives around standards of moral conduct which have been established by other people.

    One of the first official attempts at legislation intended to influence the behavior of AFDC mothers was the Notice to Law Enforcement Officials provision written into the Social Security Act in 1950. This provision, known as NOLEO, was a political response to the rising number of desertion cases among AFDC beneficiaries. [26] NOLEO required local welfare agencies to obtain the names of deserting husbands and report the information to law enforcement officials so that the deserters could be located and required to take responsibility for the children. It did not compel law enforcement agencies to act, however, and was in this respect merely a first, tentative step in developing methods of using welfare agencies as extension of other governmental agencies. It was, however, an indication that special behavior not required of persons who did not request public assistance--in this case requiring a report of desertion--would be required of AFDC recipients in the future.

The difference in beliefs between professional welfare workers and law-makers is the perspective from which the function of the welfare agency is viewed. The law-maker sees the agency as primarily a governmental agency which, by definition, should be available as an instrument to enforce compliance with society's laws. The welfare worker views the agency as being concerned with meeting the needs of people who are in need of its services. Enforcement of moral or legal standards, they argue, is the proper function of some other agency of government. As the laws are presently written, however, the former views seem to have won out. Welfare regulations are used to compel persons to adhere to certain laws--laws which many times are not enforced against the general population. An example is the enforcement of cohabitation statutes that are on the books in most states. Although most citizens need not worry, this type of statute provides officials with a vehicle to enforce a false standard of morality on persons requesting aid from the state.

Duality of the Law

An example of how a law may be more harshly applied against the poor by using welfare regulations can be seen by considering the practice of welfare searches, or "field investigations" as they are officially known.

A common practice of welfare agencies is to require recipients of AFDC benefits to agree to allow welfare workers to enter their homes so that eligibility may be confirmed. Sometimes these "field investigations" have been carried out early in the morning, in an attempt to deduce whether or not there is a man residing in the home or the mother is engaging in "immoral" or "promiscuous" behavior.

The practice of conducting mandatory "home visits" was challenged in 1971 before the Supreme Court in Wyman v. James 400 U.S. 309 (1971). [27] The challenge was based on an analogy with the cases in the criminal law field which have insisted that a governmental agent have a warrant to search a home without the owner's consent. The warrant requirement is based on the Fourth Amendment protection against unreasonable searches.

138   Social Science & Social Work

        The Court distinguished <u>Wyman</u> from the warrant
cases on the ground that there was no criminal prosecution
involved in the case, merely the cutting off of the recipient's
benefits when she failed to give her consent. It indicated
that if there was a criminal penalty involved for refusing
consent to the caseworker's "visit," the decision may have
gone the other way. Since the home-visit requirement was
"reasonable" in light of the State's "public interest" in the
welfare of the child involved, the Court upheld the state's
right to cut off aid if the AFDC recipient refused to allow
the caseworker's entry into her home.

        The Court seemed to apply an ad-hoc test of "reason-
ableness," stating that the means employed by the New York
agency were significant to the decision. There were no al-
legations of "a proposed visitation at an awkward or retirement hour ... of a forcible entry, or ... of any snooping in
the home." The recipient was given six days' advance written notice of the visitation. There were no uniformed or
police authorities involved, and the purpose was not for a
"criminal investigation."

        The Court also pointed out some "objectionable fea-
tures" of the warrant procedure that would be applicable in
the welfare area if Mrs. James' challenge were to be upheld.
These included the facts that a warrant's execution needs no
advance notice, justifies forcible entry, and its hours for
execution are not as limited as those prescribed for the home
visitations.

        Justice Douglas, in his dissent, asked whether the
government by force of its largesse had the power to "buy
up" rights guaranteed by the Constitution. "It is a strange
jurisprudence indeed which safeguards a businessman at his
place of work from warrantless searches but will not do the
same for a mother in her home," commented the Justice.

        Mr. Justice Marshall, in an opinion joined by Mr.
Justice Brennan, "emphatically disagreed" with what he considered were the three conclusions reached by the majority:
that there was no "search" involved; that even if there were
a search involved it was not "unreasonable"; and that even
if the search were unreasonable the recipient "waives her
right to object by accepting benefits."

        The welfare visit, in the words of Justice Marshall,
"is an even more severe intrusion upon privacy and family

dignity" than inspections by fire inspectors, for which the
Court had earlier required officials to obtain warrants. Re-
fusal to allow the fire inspector to enter his home had resulted in a criminal prosecution and a $100 suspended fine
to the defendant in that case. "Which result is ... more
severe, " Marshall asked, when "for protecting the privacy
of her home, Mrs. James lost the sole means of support
for herself and her infant son...?"

     The test of "reasonableness" under the Fourth Amend-
ment, as Justice Marshall pointed out, has been that any
search without a warrant is "constitutionally unreasonable... ";
not an ad-hoc consideration of the means used, absent certain specific and limited exceptions involving "exigent circumstances. "

     "Would the majority sanction, in the absence of pro-
bable cause, compulsory visits to all American homes for
the purpose of discovering child abuse?" Justice Marshall
queries. He also asks whether, as a matter of law, a poor
mother is substantially more likely to injure or exploit her
children. Possible child abuse was one of the "interests"
of the state that the majority cited as upholding its right to
insist on the visits.

     In the context of urban poverty, Marshall points out,
the majority implication that a biannual home visit assures
accurate verification of eligibility requirements "strains
credulity. " Other sources of information, such as expenditure receipts, financial records, non-home interviews, public
records, etc. , which are regularly accepted by other governmental agencies, would be much less drastic than the invasion of the privacy of the home.

     Justice Marshall, on the assertion of the rehabilitative
nature of the home visit, commented, "A paternalistic notion
that a complaining citizen's constitutional rights can be vio-
lated so long as the State is somehow helping him is alien
to our Nation's philosophy. "

     He concludes his dissent with the caustic remark: "I
find no little irony in the fact that the burden of today's departure from principled adjudication is placed upon the lowly
poor. Perhaps the majority has explained why a commercial warehouse deserves more protection than does this poor
woman's home. I am not convinced.... "

In one area of infringement upon the personal lives of welfare recipients, the Supreme Court has come to the defense of the recipient by ruling unconstitutional the residency requirements imposed by most of the states as a condition of receiving benefits. In Shapiro v. Thompson, 394 U. S. 618 (1969), the Court held those requirements to be an unconstitutional infringement upon a citizen's right to travel. Justice Jackson had spoken of a "right to travel" in a concurring opinion in Edwards v. California, 314 U. S. 160 (1941), which struck down a California "anti-Okie" statute prohibiting persons to bring indigents into the state. The majority opinion in that case, however, had rested the decision on the Commerce Clause and had not recognized a constitutional right to travel freely among the states.

Justice Brennan, who wrote the decision, thought a mother who considered the level of a state's public assistance benefits when choosing a location in which to make a new life for herself and her children to be no less deserving than a mother who moves to a particular state in order to utilize its better educational facilities.

Justices Warren and Black dissented, emphasizing that welfare recipients could travel freely from state to state and therefore there were no restrictions on travel. They indicated foreboding as to the implications of the decision toward state-imposed residency requirements dealing with eligibility to vote, participation in certain occupations or professions, and attendance at state-supported universities.

Another type of duality exists when the statutes themselves, as opposed to their enforcement, affect only the poor. Such is the case in which laws require children of needy parents to contribute any earnings to their support. The obvious duality is that children of better-off parents do not have to support their parents. On the surface this does not look like an unreasonable requirement; it may even be a practice which, in fact, is to be highly lauded. The important point is this: the practice of supporting one's needy parents may be laudable, but to legally force a child to support them discriminates against that child solely on the basis of his condition of poverty.

In Edwards v. California, Justice Jackson stated, "... 'Indigence' in itself is neither a source for rights nor a basis for denying them. The mere state of being without funds is a neutral fact--constitutionally an irrelevance, like

race, creed, or color. " If this is true, then discrimination
against the poor on the basis of their poverty, by invasion
of privacy by means of welfare search provisions, "discriminatory taxation" by means of provisions requiring the support of relatives, governmental control over personal behavior through suitable home laws, or any other such requirement, is unconstitutional and therefore illegal under the
Equal Protection Clause of the Fourteenth Amendment.   As
we have seen as recently as James v. Valtierra, supra, the
Supreme Court has not been willing to apply that clause to
welfare cases, even when they have chosen to reach the
Constitutional issues of a given case.   When the Equal Protection argument has been urged the majority of the Court
has usually found an "overriding State interest" which has
legitimized an otherwise "inherently suspect classification"
on the basis of being a recipient of welfare.   Classification
on the basis of indigency has also not fared well, except
perhaps where personal liberty has been concerned as in
Tate vs. Short, supra.

   In order successfully to challenge discriminatory legislation or welfare regulations, it is essential to try and discover why the Court has decided as it has on particular issues, and the bases it has used to justify the decisions.   In
this regard, the separate opinions delivered by the individual
Justices, whether concurring or dissenting, are often en-
lightening.

   Perhaps the most important area of inquiry is how
the case or argument was framed when presented to the
Court on appeal.   The same set of facts and circumstances
making up the case can often be argued on a variety of issues.   If a given issue, for instance Equal Protection, is
not argued at the trial level it will usually not be raisable
on appeal, even if a different counsel is arguing the case.
Therefore, it is of utmost importance for a challenge to a
discriminatory law or regulation to be based on as wide a
range of issues as may arguably be employed by the counsel
from the outset of the action.   Of course, a counsel's primary concern is his client; and he or she may have ethical
considerations if the case is framed only in broad Constitutional terms with a goal toward effecting a major policy
change, when in fact a more narrow technical attack could
be successful with less danger of a need to appeal and the
increased expenses which naturally follow.   There is no way
to predict accurately which cases may end up before the
Supreme Court and present the rare opportunity which that

circumstance affords to argue for basic policy realignments.
Every case should be built upon a base sufficiently broad to
allow the Justices an opportunity to choose a rationale in
line with their personal philosophy upon which to decide favorably the client's predicament. The technical problems
of strategy and their often unexpected ramifications are explored in some depth by Lewis in his moving book, Gideon's
Trumpet. 28 Although written in nontechnical language, the
book effectively points out and explains many of the practical
intricacies of the appeal process and, most importantly, how
unexpected developments often flavor the ultimate outcome of
a given case.

When decisions are handed down by the Supreme Court
they may easily be misinterpreted if they are not analyzed
closely. Stephan Wasby, writing in Public Welfare, 29 approaches a number of so-called "landmark decisions" affecting welfare policy with a view toward isolating the bases of
those decisions and analyzing them as to their probable effect on the policies involved. He points out that due to a
number of factors inherent in welfare cases the decisions
are often narrowly drawn, relating to statutory and regulatory interpretations rather than to broad constitutional rulings. He points to the mass of statutes and regulations in
the area as one factor limiting the scope of many decisions.
The Court will generally not reach constitutional issues (i. e. ,
invalidate a law or regulation covering an area as being
violative of a constitutional protection) when it can base its
decision on "interpreting" the language used to reach the
same result. This is especially true when dealing with Congressional enactments, since in that instance the Court is
considering the power of an "equal" branch of the government. Another reason for the lack of broad rulings in the
area is the small number of welfare cases that have reached
the Court. Perhaps additional factors are the way the cases
are presented and the nature of the rights involved as they
are seen by the Justices and by the public at large.

An example of a narrow ruling that has been popular-
ly, although erroneously, interpreted as standing for a major
shift in welfare policy is King v. Smith, 392 U. S. 309
(1968), the "man in the house" decision. The Court invalidated Alabama's "substitute-father" regulations denying AFDC
benefits to a mother who cohabitated with an able-bodied
man in or out of the home, and which applied even if the
man had no obligation to contribute to the support of the
children. The case was seen as a rebuke to this type of

social control legislation, which some consider an attempt
to enforce a different standard of morality on AFDC recipients than is enforced on the public generally.

Wasby points out, however, that the decision stands
for no such pronouncement on social control legislation. The
Alabama regulation was found inconsistent with the intent of
the Social Security Act which imposed an obligation to supply aid to families with dependent children. Chief Justice
Warren noted that, after the "Flemming Ruling" of 1961,
States could not impose eligibility criteria concerning the
"suitability" of the home. The term "parent" in the Act referred to one who had a legal obligation to contribute to the
maintenance of a child; "...destitute children who are legally
fatherless cannot be flatly denied Federally funded assistance
on the transparent fiction that they have a substitute father."
The Court thus interpreted the statute; it did not rule on the
legality of suitable home laws in general.

The rationale of King v. Smith is that a state cannot
establish a narrower basis for eligibility than the provisions
of the Social Security Act unless Congress specifically en-
ables it to. It is important to realize that no constitutional
right is involved, but rather that punitive action against
children could not be used, in violation of HEW regulations,
to control the behavior of a parent. A possible consequence
is that not only is there now an express provision for a
State cutting off aid on the basis of "unsuitability of the
home," but an argument can be made that Congress has im-
plicitly condoned taking the child away from the mother under those conditions. Whatever the intent, it is obvious
that King v. Smith has a rather limited application in the
protection of the AFDC recipient's dignity or privacy.

An important factor in trying to interpret decisions
correctly is the nature of the issues and rights that were
involved in the controversy. Necessarily this involves the
way in which the case was presented and is framed in the
record. Involved also is the way society views the "rights"
which are asserted, since society's values and biases are
often reflected in the opinions of the individual Justices who
are a product of that society.

Rights concerning personal liberty are generally considered worthy of staunch protection by both society and the
Court. Thus, we can view the decision in Tate v. Short,
supra, as a reflection of the concern involved when

imprisonment is a possible consequence. Although the Justices comprising the majority were split on the rationale to be used, the Equal Protection Clause or the Due Process Clause, the nature of the controversy was such that each agreed as to the invalidity of the practice of imprisoning defendants who lacked the funds to pay traffic fines.

Despite the intent of the framers of the Social Security Act of 1935, public assistance is viewed more as a gratuity than a right. This characterization, of course, gives the states broad latitude as to the criteria to be employed in administering their programs; and the effects of denying certain benefits to a person are not seen as sufficient justification for the Court to interfere, contrasted with the effect of denying a person his liberty, for example.

The problem, then, is to frame the issues in terms that call attention to invasions of basic personal rights in an argument which the Court is inclined to view favorably. For instance, when presenting a challenge to the discriminatory nature of a law or regulation, we know from reading prior decisions that certain facts must be known or at least argued from the trial level to establish a basis for the issues which will illicit favorable response if the case reaches the upper appellate levels or the Supreme Court. Justices Blackmun, Brennan, and Marshall have often written spirited attacks on laws which discriminate on their face against indigents as a class as being violative of the Equal Protection Clause of the Fourteenth Amendment, e. g., their dissent in James v. Valtierra, supra. But we also know that under existing precedent racial discrimination must usually be shown if a majority of the court is to be won on that argument. Therefore, a successful challenge must not only establish an equal protection argument, but must go further. It must show, for example, a lack of due process under an existing statute, as in Thorpe v. Housing Authority of Durham, 393 U.S. 268 (1969) (involving the need for pretermination hearings in eviction proceedings); or an interference with a basic personal right, as in Shapiro v. Thompson, 394 U.S. 618 (1969) (which invalidated residency requirements as infringing on an individual's right to travel). The same set of circumstances can present many different issues to a skillful attorney with the imagination and ability to prepare and present his case thoughtfully. Other persons in the helping professions have an important role too, especially in the initial stages of administrative complaints on behalf of clients.

Of course, the results of different arguments cannot be as easily predicted as this simplified analysis may seem to indicate. The individual Justices on the Court are not programmed to spew out a set response when a given button is pushed. The factual background of each case is different; and often what seem to be minor differences are controlling to a given Justice no matter how the issues are framed in argument. The important point, however, is that each case is potentially a "landmark decision," whether it starts out in the courts or in an administrative setting. Although few will ever get there, we cannot predict which ones will end up before the Supreme Court. The importance of laying a sufficient basis in the beginning stages of the litigation is obvious. We must strive toward a level of preparedness that will allow for the most effective arguments possible in those rare opportunities that do come about to effect the broad policy changes that are so obviously needed in the welfare area. Social workers and other helping service personnel may find themselves at the first step of the judicial ladder in appeals proceedings.

An example of what may have been the result of unpreparedness in this area is the decision in Wyman v. James, supra. The majority upheld the right of a state to cut off AFDC benefits to a mother who refused admission to her home to a caseworker, even though the recipient had agreed to provide the information sought if they could meet elsewhere. Since no criminal prosecution of the mother was involved, the "home visit" was not considered the equivalent of a "search." The state was "fulfilling a public trust" in checking on the well-being of the dependant child, and therefore had a "sufficient interest" to insist on the visit as a condition to eligibility. The opinions of both the majority and the dissent center around Fourth Amendment arguments dealing with the mother's right to be free from "unreasonable searches" by the State. As Judge Nanette Dembitz has asserted, the Court ignored perhaps the most important issue of the case; the right of a child to proper care (as asserted in King v. Smith, supra) rather than the rights of the mother. 30

Policy Discussion Issues

The "Law"--Two Viewpoints

        When the average white, middle-class American
thinks of the "law" he is probably either annoyed at the
"pickiness" of a traffic cop, pleased that he has found a
loop-hole in the income-tax regulations, or outraged at the
lack of "law and order" that he is witnessing on the evening
news. Outside of tax regulations, he probably never sees
the law as an enemy to be avoided. His home is never
searched at two o'clock in the morning for signs of irregular
behavior, his income is seldom taken away because he has
been involved in an illicit affair with a woman, and if he de-
cides that another state would provide him with a better opportunity for financial success there is nothing stopping him
from moving. Outside of severe physical harm he can
usually treat his children in any manner he sees fit. He
can leave them alone every day, discipline them severely
or not discipline them at all, see to their every need or
only to the most essential requirements--all usually without
the slightest risk of having them taken away by the courts.
If this middle-class person is a woman, she can live with
any number of boyfriends, have any number of illegitimate
children, or keep any company she wishes without much
fear of intervention by a public agency.

        If our middle-class citizen is ever arrested, he will
probably view the bail system as a way to get out of jail
in order to prepare an adequate defense. His lawyer will
be free to give him as much time and effort as is needed
to handle his case adequately. The judge and jury will probably not hold any particular biases against him in determining his guilt or innocence, or the sentence to be given him.

        If this same person were poor and of minority class
status, or merely poor alone, all of the above would be un-
true. Former Attorney General Katzenbach has described
the difference in this way: "To us (the 'comfortable' as opposed to the 'poor'), laws and regulations are protections
and guides, established for our benefit, and for us to use.
But to the poor they are a hostile maze, established as harassment, at all costs to be avoided ... Small wonder then
that the poor man does not respect the law. He has little
reason to believe it is his guardian; he has every reason to
believe it is an instrument of the ... well off ... we make

him a functional outlaw."[31] Attorney General Robert Kennedy commented when discussing the difference: "The poor man looks upon the law as an enemy, not as a friend. For him the law is always taking something away."[32]

What Can Be Done

It is not enough merely to point out the inequities which exist in our system. If the unequal treatment relating to the operation of the criminal justice system is, as most recent studies have indicated, linked to poverty in only an indirect and non-causal relationship, then perhaps we can improve that situation by studying some of the other factors involved. For instance, if judges sentence poor people more severely than middle-class persons, not because of their poverty but because there is something about not making bail which influences decisions in that way, then the answer may lie in finding a bail system which allows the poor person to be freed on some more equitable criteria than possessing the needed funds or collateral. The Manhattan Bail Project[33] found this to be the case. The persons released in that experiment were judged mainly on the basis of their "roots" in the community rather than the money they could put up when under consideration for bail. Persons who had families or relatives in the community, who had jobs, who had lived there for at least six months, and who were notified clearly of the date, time, and place of their expected appearance were found to be excellent risks. The results of their trials and sentencing were found to be similar to those of persons financially able to make the regular bail, both of which were significantly better for the defendant than those of persons not able to make bail. The new Florida system of "Pre-Trial Release" is an example of what some states have been recently considering as alternatives to the set bail schedules that are generally in use. At this writing, however, it is too early to evaluate its effect.

In the same vein, if it is not poverty but lack of adequate services from legal counsel that causes some of the discrimination, the solution may be to provide for more lawyers in the Public Defender offices in order to allow each lawyer to spend more time and effort on a client's case. OEO legal services is an example of a federal program enacted toward that end.

As stated before, when the prejudicial treatment is

not knowingly intended as discrimination against the poor the
solutions seem fairly obvious, needing only study and effort
to implement despite the problem of implementing new sub-
systems in our judicial system. When the discrimination is
specifically intended, however, as it is in the case of social-
control legislation, the problem becomes much more difficult. The problem becomes one of changing people's out-
looks and beliefs rather than changing procedures in a system's operation. It deals with emotions and prejudice rather
than the more tangible subjects of criteria for bail or the
caseload of public defenders. It requires a judgment as to
the "rightness" or "wrongness" of controling the personal
lives of welfare recipients, as opposed to merely finding a
solution to a situation which nearly everyone already agrees
ought to be changed at least on principle.

When we deal with the "morality" of a subject we are
dealing with a highly abstract, personalized concept which
can be defined differently by any two persons viewing it.

Social-control legislation identifies the welfare recipient as unable to make it in our society on his own and
brands him as "inferior" for being in that state. It recog-
nizes that society has a certain responsibility, at least from
a paternalistic point of view, especially if the inability is
due to factors outside of that person's control. Even so,
the recipient of public funds must make certain non-economic
sacrifices to qualify him to be kept even at the lowest possible level of existence; he must be "worthy" of help. If a
physical handicap prevents him from being self-supporting,
especially blindness or a war injury (something easily recog-
nizable), his sacrifice is considered made. If lack of sal-
able skills, useful education, or too many children are the
reason, however, something extra must be exacted from
him. He must consent to humiliating investigations, invasion of his privacy, regulation of his personal behavior, inferences concerning his reliability and ability to "handle
money," and a host of other demeaning practices which de-
stroy self-respect and rob him of his personal freedom.
The rest of society may deviate from the ideals set forth
concerning the "right" type of behavior; but the poor must
toe a more rigid line.

Aside from the fact that they do not accomplish their
goals, social-control attempts by legislators contradict the
concepts which are the basis for our society: reasonable
personal freedom and the right to personal dignity. As to

practice, the worker stressing broker and advocate roles
needs a general knowledge of welfare law and legal procedures.   Such basic knowledge will provide greater effectiveness in the use of legal aid resources.

Notes

1.   John M. Martin and Joseph P. Fitzpatrick, Delinquent
      Behavior--A Redefinition of the Problem (New York,
      Random House, 1965), p. 26.

2.   Ibid., p. 27.

3.   Ibid., p. 27.

4.   Don C. Gibbons, Delinquent Behavior (Englewood Cliffs:
      Prentice-Hall, Inc., 1970), p. 50.

5.   In re Gault 387 U.S. 1 (1967).

6.   Ibid., pp. 36-39.

7.   Ibid., pp. 40-42.

8.   Ibid., p. 41.

9.   Ibid., p. 58.

10.   Martin and Fitzpatrick, op. cit., p. 29.

11.   Charles E. Ares, et al., "The Manhattan Bail Pro-
      ject," The Sociology of Punishment and Correction,
      Norman Johnston, et al., eds. (New York, John
      Wiley and Sons, Inc., 1970), p. 148.

12.   Ibid., p. 148.

13.   Ibid., p. 149.

14.   Ibid., pp. 157-158.

15.   372 U.S. 335 (1963).

16.   384 U.S. 436 (1966).

17.   Richard H. Seeburger and R. Stanton Wettick, Jr.,

"The Miranda Decision: Effects on Confessions and
Convictions," The Sociology of Punishment and Correction, op. cit., p. 115.

18. Presentation by Robert McLure, President of the Tallahassee Legal Aid Society, at the American Civil
Liberties Union Sponsored panel discussion of "Legal
Rights of the Poor," Florida State University, February 25, 1971.

19. See Carol Heet Katz, editor, The Law and the Low Income Consumer, Project on Social Welfare Law,
Supplement 2, New York Law School, 1968.

20. See Clearinghouse Review, 3, April, 1970, pp. 333-334.

21. See Clearinghouse Review, 6, July, 1972, p. 178.

22. See Clearinghouse Review, 5, August-September, 1971,
p. 273.

23. Patricia M. Wald, "Poverty and Criminal Justice,"
The Sociology of Punishment and Corrections, et
al., eds. (New York: John Wiley and Sons, 1970),
pp. 271-296.

24. Gilbert Steiner, Social Insecurity: The Politics of Welfare, Chicago: Rand McNally, 1966, pp. 108-140.

25. Ibid., p. 113.

26. Ibid., p. 114.

27. See Stephen L. Wasby, "Welfare Policy and the Supreme
Court," Public Welfare, 3, 2, Spring, 1972, for a
discussion of Wyman vs. James. We are much in-
debted to Professor Wasby for the general tone of
his discussion which we have enlarged.

28. Anthony Lewis, Gideon's Trumpet (New York: Vintage
Books--Alfred A. Knopf, Inc., 1964).

29. Wasby, op. cit., pp. 16-27.

30. Nanette Dembitz, "Welfare Home Visits: Child Versus
Parents," American Bar Association Journal, 57,
(September, 1971), pp. 371-374.

31. Albert M. Bendich, "Privacy, Poverty, and the Con-
     stitution," in The Law and the Poor, Jacobus ten
     Broek, ed. (San Francisco: Chandler Publishing
     Company, 1966), pp. 99-100.

32. Ibid.

33. Ares, op. cit., pp. 146-166.

11. SURVEY OF UNMET MEDICAL NEEDS OF CHILDREN IN SIX COUNTIES IN FLORIDA*

A survey of unmet medical needs of children under 16 years old in six counties of Florida--Leon, Gadsden, Jefferson, Franklin, Wakulla, and Liberty--was undertaken in 1967. The study was aimed primarily at uncovering prevalent diseases and other health conditions and determining whether the affected children were receiving adequate treatment. A secondary purpose was to obtain a general description of community medical services and to appraise their adequacy.

As a basis for comparison, general demographic data were collected from the 1900 U. S. census, official reports of the State, county health departments, public schools, and public welfare agencies. Special attention was given to medical records of Head Start children in three counties participating in the Head Start program in 1966. Interviews were planned for a sample apportioned according to the child population reported for each of the six counties in the 1960 census. On this basis, the samples from each county were 50 percent in Leon, 31 percent in Gadsden, 8 percent in Jefferson, 4.3 percent in Franklin, 4 percent in Wakulla, and 2.4 percent in Liberty.

Adequacy of medical care was evaluated in terms of money being spent by various public agencies for service to the families who could not purchase medical care. Annual income data were obtained so that correlations could be made with health problems and income levels and samples could be evaluated according to the 1960 census income distribution in the six counties.

*Reproduced from Public Health Reports, Public Health Service, U. S. Department of Health, Education and Welfare, v. 85, no. 3, March 1970, pp. 189-196.

General Demographic Data

     In 1960 the nonwhite population was approximately 60 percent in Gadsden County, 60 percent in Jefferson County, 33 percent in Leon County, 28 percent in Wakulla County, 21 percent in Franklin County, and 15 percent in Liberty County. In the entire State of Florida, 18 percent of the population was nonwhite.

     Of the six counties, all but Leon had a larger number of children than the State's average. Also, a comparatively heavy concentration of aged persons in Franklin and Jefferson Counties resulted in a greater dependency rate. In 1960 Florida contained a higher percentage of persons over age 65 compared to the United States as a whole, and Franklin County exceeded the State rate.

     All but Leon County had a median income below the State average. The 1960 census indicated that more than half of the families had incomes less than $3,000 per year in Franklin, Gadsden, Jefferson, and Wakulla Counties. Baseline income data are shown in table 1.

     Dire poverty was evident in all but Leon County in 1960. The percentage of families with less than $1,000 income were 15.5 in Wakulla, 12.9 in Jefferson, 12.1 in Franklin, 10.4 in Liberty, 10.3 in Gadsden, and 6.5 in Leon.

Table 1. Median and high-low income distributions, 1960 census

Location	Median income	Percent families with incomes of	
		$3,000 or less	$10,000 or more
United States-------------	$5,560	21.4	15.1
State of Florida-----------	4,722	28.4	11.1
Counties of Florida:			
Franklin----------------	2,699	56.7	1.5
Gadsden----------------	2,866	52.5	6.0
Jefferson--------------	2,741	54.4	4.9
Liberty----------------	3,277	46.2	.5
Leon------------------	5,173	27.3	13.6
Wakulla---------------	2,783	54.3	3.3

In 1967 infant death rates exceeded the State average
only in Gadsden County and the national average (22.1) only
in Franklin and Gadsden Counties as compared to 1964 when
Franklin, Gadsden, Jefferson, and Leon Counties exceeded
State and national averages.   Marked declines occurred in
Gadsden, Jefferson, and Leon Counties between 1961 and
1967 (table 2).

The following total death rates were recorded for
persons under age 20 in 1967 (1):   Franklin 3, Gadsden 38,
Jefferson 11, Leon 67, Liberty 2, and Wakulla 5.   The infant deaths equaled childhood and youth deaths, ages 1 to 20.
Apparently existent health problems did not lead to a large
number of deaths during childhood.   Thus, we examined
Head Start medical records and survey findings with a view
to conditions which limit child development and mental and
physical effectiveness in adulthood.

Methodology

Two approaches were used in the study.   The first
was a review of the medical examination records of the Head
Start children who were enrolled in summer 1966.   We reviewed all available records for these children in Franklin
County, every fifth record in several schools in Leon County, and every fourth record in Jefferson County.   This sample was somewhat biased because the Head Start children's
families had to have an income of less than $3,000 per
year.   A further limitation was that physical examination
records for most of the Head Start children were incomplete.   The physicians left many items blank on the forms,
and it was difficult to know how to interpret these blanks.

The second approach was to interview families in the
six counties concerning immunizations and health problems
of children under age 16.   The questionnaire included family
income, race, vaccinations for smallpox and poliomyelitis,
and DTP immunization.   Also included were questions concerning whether during the past year the child had seen a
physician or dentist, or both, and whether he had:

Unexplained loss of weight.
Eating problems.
unexplained tiredness, regularly.
Running ear--watery, bloody, pus.
Poor vision--either for distance or for close work

Table 2. Infant death rates per 1,000 live births, by race and by county of residence in 1961 and 1967, Florida

County	Infant deaths, 1961			Infant deaths, 1967		
	Total	White	Nonwhite	Total	White	Nonwhite
State totals	29.1	23.2	45.8	23.8	18.8	37.1
Franklin	23.5	23.6	23.3	23.6	[1] 22.0	[1] 27.8
Gadsden	60.9	33.6	69.2	30.3	[1] 9.8	[1] 36.8
Jefferson	39.2	15.4	47.4	21.2	[1] 18.9	22.1
Leon	32.2	20.2	53.6	16.6	12.4	25.3
Liberty	23.3	29.4	[1] .0	[1] 18.9	[1] 20.8	[1] .0
Wakulla	17.7	13.3	26.3	19.0	[1] 14.4	[1] 26.3

[1]Based on less than 100 live births.

SOURCES: Florida State Board of Health, annual reports, Jacksonville, 1962, p. 76; 1968, p. 327.

such as reading.
Persistent headaches.
Toothache or unable to chew food.
Persistent skin rashes or itching of skin--"breaking
out. "
Persistent pains in chest.
Persistent cough (except chest colds).
Severe shortness of breath after doing light work.
Coughing up or spitting blood.
Repeated or persistent backache.
Persistent pains in joints.
Open or running sores or boils that do not heal any-
where on the body.
Repeated vomiting, several days or more.
Repeated or prolonged pains in stomach or anywhere
in abdomen.
"Rupture"--hernia or wearing of truss.
Fainting spells, stuttering, stammering, nervous
breakdown, "fits" or convulsions.
Accidental injuries--broken bones, head injuries, ac-
cidental poisoning, snake bites, or other types of
injury.

Four students who were majoring in social welfare
were selected to do the interviewing. They were oriented
as to the purpose of the study and interview procedure which
included exploration of the respondent's understanding of the
questions. The interview schedule was adapted from an approach devised by Hoffer and associates of Michigan State
College[2,3]. Several changes were made to tailor the schedule to children. When the medical needs schedule was used
in Michigan, the effectiveness of the interview approach was
evaluated by examination of a sample of the interviewees by
personnel of the University of Michigan School of Medicine.

The Michigan interview approach was determined to
be 80 percent effective; 10 percent of its failure resulted
from missing significant symptoms and 10 percent from
over-reading of symptoms. Because no similar medical
examination arrangement was possible in our study, we could
not expect the high percentage of effectiveness attained in
Michigan.

I believe that medical needs may have been understated in our study because of the more limited education of
our interviewees, compared to those in Michigan, and because of communication problems between interviewers and

interviewees. For our study, health conditions were analyzed according to age, race, and income at the Florida
State University Computer Center.

Results

Head Start medical records. The Head Start children's medical records in the three participating counties,
except for those in Jefferson and the village of Carrabelle
in Franklin County, generally were incomplete and ambiguous
as to whether a health problem did not exist or was ignored.
Some inconsistencies were also seen in the medical report
forms used. Because of the differences in the forms, only
tooth decay and immunizations could be reported generally.

Of the Head Start children for whom dental examinations were recorded, 87 percent in Franklin, 97 percent in
Jefferson, 39 percent in Leon, and 70 percent of the total
number examined needed dental care. This need may have
been understated because the records in Leon County were
less complete than in the other two counties.

The immunization records indicated that 33 percent
of the Head Start children had not been vaccinated against
smallpox. In Leon County only 45 percent were reported to
have had DTP and only 40 percent had received polio vaccine.

A high incidence of hypochromic anemia was seen in
two counties--10 of 27 children in Carrabelle and 10 of 31
children in Jefferson County were reported to have this condition.

Family interviews. Interviews were conducted with
389 families, having a total of 1,177 children, in the six
counties. The sample was skewed toward the low-income
group, because 43.3 percent of the children were in families
having incomes of less than $3,000 per year. Among the
six counties, the percentages of families in this income
group exceeded the percentages reported in the 1960 census
in all but Franklin and Jefferson Counties.

All health conditions listed in the questionnaire drew
some response. The lowest count was 12 each for backache
and hernia. Complaints reported by more than 4 percent of
the total were eating problems, 24 percent; cavities, 21

percent; skin rash, 12 percent; injuries or poisoning, 11
percent; vision difficulties, 10 percent; headache, 8 percent;
ear trouble, 6.3 percent; repeatedly occurring stomach
pains, 6 percent; running sores and boils, 5 percent; fainting spells and speech problems, 5 percent; and unexplained
tiredness, 4 percent. Untreated conditions, including the
eating problem, were reported for 34 percent of the children. Excluding the eating problem, 26 percent of the children had untreated conditions.

Of the children with untreated health conditions, 57.5
percent were in families with incomes less than $3,000 per
year (43.3 percent of all the children were in this income
group). Untreated conditions were reported for 33 percent
of the children in families with less than $1,000 income,
40 percent in the $1,000-$2,000 bracket, and 32 percent in
the $2,000-$3,000 bracket.

A significant difference in chances of treatment according to race was indicated (table 3). The percentage
calculations were based on the total number of children included in the interviews in the six counties and the total
numbers of white and nonwhite children in each county. For
example, the basis for comparison for all six counties in
table 3 was 1,177 children, 524 white and 653 nonwhite.

The questionnaire responses suggested that the nonwhite children had less chance of being immunized than the
white children. The comparative percentages of nonim-
munized children were as follows:

Disease	White	Nonwhite
Smallpox-----------------	27	35
Diphtheria, tetanus, and pertussis---------------	17	33
Poliomyelitis-------------	16	26

These percentages indicate that the immunization failure reported in the records of Head Start children for diptheria,
tetanus, and pertussis and poliomyelitis may be accurate
because the majority of these children were from low-income
nonwhite families. Of the total numbers of white and nonwhite children, 32 percent had not been vaccinated against
smallpox, 25 percent had not received DTP, and 22 percent
had not received poliomyelitis vaccine. As to age division,
20 percent of those under age 7 and 11 percent of those

Table 3. Percentage of children in families having less than $3,000 annual income with untreated and treated health problems, by race, six counties in Florida, 1966

County	All children		Untreated		Treated[1]	
	Number	Percent below $3,000	White	Nonwhite	White	Nonwhite
Franklin--------------	61	42.6	47.0	55.5	23.5	22.2
Gadsden--------------	372	55.6	14.0	36.5	71.0	25.5
Jefferson------------	102	52.0	(2)	31.0	(2)	42.2
Leon-----------------	561	30.0	18.2	31.3	45.5	35.3
Liberty--------------	30	70.0	28.6	25.0	14.3	(2)
Wakulla--------------	51	63.0	(2)	51.6	100.0	3.0
Total--------------	1,177	43.3	30.0	35.4	31.6	30.0

[1] At least 1 health condition treated.

[2] No health problems reported.

Table 4. Percentages of 18-month-old children immunized against selected diseases, 1968

County[1]	All[2]	Smallpox (1 dose)	Poliomyelitis		DTP		None
			(2 or more doses)	(1 or more doses)	(3 or more doses)	(1 or more doses)	
State--------	25.4	34.7	69.8	80.6	69.7	82.4	15.4
Franklin------	3.8	9.5	45.7	65.1	42.9	67.6	22.7
Gadsden------	42.4	46.1	64.5	76.4	63.2	76.0	34.2
Leon--------	12.3	24.5	56.0	73.8	56.4	74.5	24.5
Liberty-------	43.5	32.2	95.7	97.8	95.7	97.8	2.2
Wakulla------	4.3	6.5	32.6	44.6	32.6	48.9	46.7

[1]Jefferson County did not report for 1968.

[2]Measles vaccination included as well as smallpox, poliomyelitis, and DTP.

SOURCE: Florida State Board of Health, annual report, Jacksonville, 1968, derived from table 29, p. 235.

aged 7 and above were not protected against smallpox, 16 percent of those under age 7 and 9 percent of those aged 7 and above had not received DTP, and 15 percent under age 7 and 7 percent aged 7 and above were not protected against poliomyelitis.

An immunization program, partially supported by a grant from the Public Health Service, functioned between 1963 and 1968. Results have not been very encouraging (table 4).

Public Medical Expenditures

The Florida State Department of Public Welfare began to pay for prescribed medicines in April 1966. All counties in the State were making some use of this Federal-State option. In the six counties studied, assistance was being given to a monthly average of 25 families at an average cost of $8.36.

The State made limited use of the vendor payment program. In fall 1965 the average vendor payment per child under Aid to Families with Dependent Children (AFDC) was $3.15 for the nation and 45 cents for Florida. The average annual hospital payment for AFDC children in Florida was $8.50; in the six counties it was $4.43 per child. None of these payments were made in Wakulla County. Participation in the prescribed medicine part of the Federal State vendor program was about the same for the six counties as for the State. The average monthly payment per AFDC child was 26 cents in these counties and 25 cents in the State.

County health department expenditures were largely directed toward immunizations. Limited expenditures were made for direct treatment of sores, hookworm, pediculosis, tuberculosis, and venereal disease. For other conditions, referral was made to private physicians. County health units were spending about $10.60 per capita. Only Leon County had a Federal grant, in the amount of $12,873, during fiscal year 1964. Recent reports of the Florida State Board of Health reflect inadequate functioning of county health departments in terms of the number of indigent children receiving medical service as compared to an estimate of the number needing service. [4a]

The ratio of need to intake for county health department medical services was stated as follows:

County	Intake	Ratio
State total-----------------	15,473	48.1
Franklin-------------------	5	5.8
Gadsden-------------------	308	62.7
Jefferson-----------------	8	6.6
Leon----------------------	69	13.6
Liberty-------------------	3	11.1
Wakulla-------------------	11	18.0

County welfare was a limited medical care resource
in 1966. Welfare expenditures were approximately
$46,340,000, 30 percent of the total State welfare expendi-
tures. Of this amount, $38,476,000 was for medical ex-
penditures. County expenditures were even more limited in
the six counties. For example, an annual report of the
Associated Charities of Leon County, financed by city and
county funds and by private donation, reported a total annual
budget of $43,393.80; an administrative cost of $28,240.40
left only $15,103.40 for services for a population of about
100,000.

A total of 783 families were receiving direct welfare
in Leon County in 1966--assistance for food, medicine, physicians' fees, fuel, transportation, rent, utilities, and nursing home care. Among the 783 families were 36 white and
77 nonwhite families whose applications for welfare were rejected. Assistance was given to 74 white and 70 nonwhite
families in purchasing medicines. Additional medical aid
was given to 24 white and 31 nonwhite families.

The Florida Crippled Children's Commission provided
services for 649 eligible children in the six counties during
the fiscal year ending 1966.

The records of county health departments revealed
some common health problems in children as well as preventive activities. The incidence of intestinal parasites was
particularly high in Gadsden County--5,294 of 39,424 persons
with intestinal parasites treated in the State were treated in
this county in 1966.[5] Gadsden County was more active than
Leon County in providing immunization and vaccination for
diphtheria, whooping cough, tetanus, and smallpox in relation
to the total population.

All six counties had physical examination programs for 1,458 school children in 1967, but the low rate of referrals completed (5 percent) suggested a lack of facilities or effort. This impression was supported by the fact that 50 percent of the referrals were completed for the entire State. [4b]

School children, aged 5-17 years, in Liberty and Wakulla Counties received dental examinations in 1965. In Liberty County, 227 of 319 children examined needed dental care and in Wakulla County 53 of 55 examined needed such care.

In Liberty County the 227 children needing dental care constituted 27 percent of the total children aged 5-17 years enrolled in school in 1965. The 53 children in Wakulla County represented 4 percent of the 5-17 age group enrolled in school. Of course, it cannot be assumed that all children not examined in these counties had good teeth, but for the 27 percent in Liberty County who needed dental care there were no reports of referrals.

A 32 percent successful referral rate for children with hearing problems and a 48 percent successful referral rate for children with vision difficulties suggested a lack of resources or a failure in referral efforts for the six counties in 1967. [4b]

Health Programs and Agencies

The study revealed a number of gaps in the public effort to provide the health services needed by the children in low-income families in 1966. The following is a partial list.

1. Public assistance grants were far too low to permit adequate food, shelter, and clothing. The average AFDC payment per recipient for these purposes was $15.38 in Florida in September 1966 and $20.55 in May 1969.

2. The State of Florida had only limited participation in the Federal-State grants-in-aid medical services program, and the Medicaid program had not yet been started. (The Medicaid program, which was activated January 1, 1970, provides little improvement. Coverage is limited to requirements under title XIX and so the medically indigent,

nonwelfare recipient category is excluded. Physician services up to 12 visits a year were authorized, but it is anticipated that funds appropriated will not last until July 1, 1970. Also included were per-year authorization of inpatient hospital services up to 45 days, outpatient services up to $100, and laboratory and X-ray services up to $50. Maximums for skilled nursing homes and prescribed drugs were set at $300 and $20 per month respectively. The State will not spend appreciably more, the counties will spend less, and the additional Federal funds are not sufficient to greatly improve medical and hospital services.)

3. Although county health departments scored some important gains over the past decade, some limitations were apparent. For example, in Leon County a well-staffed health department indicated that it could provide only limited medical treatment, such as for intestinal parasites and venereal disease, and suggested that low-income persons see private physicians for other health problems. Immunizations could be obtained only on certain days, and there was only a moderate immunization program through the schools or through home visits by nurses. Immunizations appeared to be more thorough in Liberty and Gadsden Counties where there were some reports of exception to a basic poor law attitude in reaching out to provide preventive medical services.

4. Direct welfare provided limited funds for medical care, as in the example cited earlier regarding the Leon County Associated Charities.

5. School health records generally showed inadequate medical service and poor recordkeeping when physicians did give examinations.

6. The medical-social work function of helping people, which makes constructive use of the limited medical services available, was lacking.

7. Citizens in general had limited faith in the growing concept of the value of the larger investment in human resources through health and educational programs by the community, State, and nation.

8. The humane interest in providing for those needing help did not adequately substitute for lag in the more selfish community tax cost versus service gain justification.

Summary

A study undertaken in 1967 to ascertain the amount of unmet medical needs of children under age 16 in six counties of Florida--Leon, Franklin, Gadsden, Jefferson, Liberty, and Wakulla--revealed that low family incomes, compared to averages in the State and the nation, and relatively high dependency ratios severely limited family capacity to purchase medical services.

Two avenues of investigation were used. Head Start medical records were reviewed in the three counties sponsoring Head Start programs, and 389 families in the six counties, having a total of 1,177 children, were interviewed regarding immunizations and health conditions of the children. Additional information was obtained from reports of the Florida State Board of Health and other public agencies.

Although infant mortality rates had declined from 1960 to 1967, many serious gaps in child health care were apparent: (a) 70 percent of the Head Start children were in need of dental care, (b) hypochromic anemia was common, (c) more than half of the Head Start children were not immunized against smallpox, diphtheria, tetanus, pertussis, and poliomyelitis, (d) a third of the children in the interview survey had health conditions which indicated need for examination by a physician or dentist, (e) a third of the interview children had not been vaccinated against smallpox and a fourth were not protected against diphtheria, tetanus, pertussis, or poliomyelitis, (f) nonwhite children had appreciably less medical care than white children, and (g) public medical services were more limited than State or national averages in terms of services available and per patient expenditures. Subsequent reports by the State board of health supported findings of inadequate medical care in the area studied.

Notes

1. Florida State Board of Health. Florida Vital Statistics. Jacksonville, Bureau of Vital Statistics, 1967, p. 34.

2. Hoffer, C. R., et al. Health Needs and Health Care in Michigan. East Lansing, Michigan State College Special Bulletin 365, c. 1949 (data presented for 1948).

3. Hoffer, C. R., and Jane, C. Health Needs and Health

Care in Two Selected Michigan Communities.   Pamphlet.   East Lansing, Michigan State College Agricultural Experiment Station, 1952.

4. Florida State Board of Health.   Annual Report.   Jacksonville, 1968, (a) p. 222; (b) appendix table 26.

5. Florida State Board of Health.   Annual Report.   Jacksonville, 1966, p. 146.

12. THE VOUCHER DAY-CARE SYSTEM*

The fragmentation and failures of the income maintenance and social services systems which have been described have produced interest in trying to use autonomous market forces as a means of developing greater effectiveness in the distribution of welfare money and social services. For example, in Florida, some legislators, who lacked confidence in the Division of Family Service of the Department of Health and Rehabilitative Services, have recommended that some private organization, such as the Retail Credit Association, be employed to check client eligibility rather than using state-employed social workers. A pilot study, completed in November, 1972, indicated the same unit cost, $10 per review, with no apparent improvement in efficiency. In addition, the Retail Credit Association sought information from neighbors and others, and, although such practices are increasingly common in the building of governmental dossiers on the non-poor, social work principles have not traditionally condoned such practice.

As the "workfare instead of welfare" hue and cry has permeated presidential, congressional, and legislative halls as a solution to "the welfare problem," it has become apparent that extensive and costly day-care services will have to be arranged if more AFDC mothers are to be pushed into the labor market. Many are already there, but the desire for control and the use of authority is strong, despite Leonard Goodwin's Brookings Institution report which found the work ethic to be just as strong for AFDC Work Incentive Program recipients as for the non-poor labor market participant.[1] The proposed voucher day-care system could be used either in a climate of voluntarism with opportunities provided for work, or in an atmosphere of coercion with or without concern for work opportunity, so leaving a greater

*Published with the permission of the principal author, Philip L. Andrew, MSW, Lynn County, Iowa, Mental Health Center.

choice to the consumer of services. A brief, heuristic, but
systemic format illustrates the application of social science
knowledge and techniques to problem solving. A voucher
day-care system might prove to be the most acceptable solution to the day-care problem in light of existing values.

The Problem

     In the past, several traditional sources have served
as the day-care network in this country. In 1965 the United
States Children's Bureau conducted a survey to assess what
type of care children were receiving in the absence of their
mothers. Some of the findings of that survey are as follows: 1) the greatest number of children, or about sixty
per cent, are cared for in their own homes, usually by relatives; 2) another twenty-five per cent are cared for outside
their own homes by relatives, friends or babysitters; 3) only
about six per cent of the children under six are exposed to
any organized day-care facility; and 4) approximately eight
per cent of all children between six and eleven, or 480,000
children, receive no supervision in the absence of their
mothers. [2]

     In the past twenty-five years, several important so-
cial and economic changes have placed increasing demands
on this informal day-care network. Chief among these
changes has been the increasing utilization of women with
children in the labor market. In 1964, thirty-four per cent
of the labor force was composed of women, 3.6 million of
whom had children under age six. [3] This figure had doubled
since 1950. At the present time, over twenty-one million
children under age fifteen have working mothers. [4] Six million of these children are under school age, thus requiring
full-time day-care services in the absence of their mothers. [5]
Despite the large number of children needing day-care services, the total capacity of licensed day-care facilities in
the United States in 1962 was only 185,000. [6]

     This lack of adequate day-care facilities is particular-
ly acute among the poor and minority groups. Kadushin
states that forty-six per cent of husbandless women with
children under six are employed. [7] Thus, as divorce, separation and illegitimacy rates increase, more women will be
employed, with a resultant increase in day-care needs.
Black mothers are particularly in need of day-care services.
Thirty per cent of black mothers with children under age

three, and fifty per cent with children between the ages of
three and five are employed. [8] However, these groups of
mothers are frequently the least able to afford adequate day-
care for their children. A 1962 Children's Bureau survey
found that eighty-three per cent of all children with employed
mothers, where the mother is the sole support, come from
families with annual incomes under $4,000. [9]

Governmental response to increases in day-care needs
have been periodic and piecemeal at best. When the government has acted, it has generally been in response to adult
needs rather than those of children. During the Civil War
and the Depression, the federal government did fund limited
day-care services. The greatest federal venture into this
area was conducted during World War II under the Lanham
Act. [10] This Act provided for funds to the states on a fifty-
fifty matching basis for the development of group day-care
facilities. At its highest point of operation, 1,600,000 children were served by this network. However, at the conclusion of the War the Act was repealed because of a perceived lack of continued need. Again in 1962 the federal
structure did provide some funds for day care through the
Title V Amendments to the Social Security Act. However,
the main thrust of this Act was to provide day-care services to welfare recipients seeking educational or employment opportunities. [11] It was not designed to implement a
comprehensive system of day-care services for all employed
mothers.

Goals and Objectives

The general purpose of this discussion will be to devise a system, the goal of which will be to utilize the disciplines of health, education and social work in meeting the
day-care needs of working mothers and their children.

The specific objectives of this day care system will
be:

1. to decrease the number of children presently receiving unsupervised or inadequate day care in the
absence of their working mothers;

2. to provide preschool children with an educational
program which will better prepare them for entry
into the school system and which will supplement the

educational experiences of children already in school;

3. to provide preventive health care measures such as immunizations, physical examinations and dietary supplements to help insure the physical development of the children served;

4. to act as a referral service to other community agencies such as the mental health center, the welfare department, child guidance centers, etc., for families where such services seem appropriate and are requested.

Alternative Solutions

There are several possible alternate solutions which could meet the stated objectives of this system. First, the federal government could encourage employers through tax benefits to develop day-care facilities for the children of their employees. Industries that employ large numbers of women could institute such a program on the premises of the work facility. Smaller businesses could cooperatively form a day-care program for their employees. However, this approach would have several limitations. First, large numbers of women live a considerable distance from their place of employment and travel to work in car pools, on buses or other public transportation facilities. It would be impractical to suggest that these women could take their children with them. Secondly, this solution would not provide day care for those mothers employed by individual families as housekeepers, cooks or in other domestic occupations.

A second possible solution would be the development of child care centers by state and local governments with federal financial backing. This approach is typified by the Universal Child Care and Development Act introduced into the Congress by Senators Bayh and Mondale.[12] This Act would have authorized the establishment of public agencies named "Child Service Districts" in each state that submitted an acceptable day-care plan to the Secretary of Health, Education and Welfare. Under the provisions of the Act all children within a district, from infancy to age fourteen, would be eligible for its services. This approach also has certain limitations. First, because of its broad scope, this program would be tremendously expensive. There are

presently twenty-one million children under fifteen whose
mothers are employed. [13] The costs of providing services
to that many children would almost certainly make it politically unfeasible at this time. Secondly, it is probable that
many Americans would oppose such massive governmental
involvement in the raising of children. Of similar proposals,
the conservative columnist, James J. Kilpatrick has said,
"In the context of a Sovietized society, in which children are
regarded as wards of the state and raised in state-controlled
communes, the scheme would make beautiful sense."[14]

A third possible solution which may prove to be the
most practical, would be the provision of vouchers with
which working mothers could purchase day-care services.
These vouchers would be issued to mothers on the basis of
their income, the number of children they have, and the
hours of day-care service required. The vouchers could be
utilized at any private day-care service which met the criteria established by law.

Assumptions, Constraints and Resources
_____

The utilization of such a voucher system to meet the
day-care needs of working mothers would rest on several
important assumptions. First, it is assumed that private
enterprise would respond to this new market and adequately
increase the number of day-care facilities. Recent increases
in the number of private nursing homes in response to Medicaid and Medicare seem to justify this assumption. Secondly, it is assumed that there would exist sufficient competition among these private day-care centers to insure that they
would be responsive to the social, health and educational
needs of the particular areas they served. Third, such a
voucher system would rest on the assumption that parents
could effectively discriminate between the various centers
and choose the one most suitable for their child's needs.
As Rivlin has pointed out, the major problem with a voucher
system is consumer ignorance about the quality of the service purchased. [15] Finally, it is assumed that these private
centers could be adequately monitored to insure compliance
with statutory standards.

In all probability, the major constraint on developing
such a system would be the enormous costs. According to
the Children's Bureau, the average cost to maintain a child
in day care full-time, five days a week, fifty-two weeks per

year, is $1,000 annually.[16] The total cost of the system
would depend on how high or low a ceiling is placed on the
family's income to qualify for the voucher. A second constraint on the implementation of such a system might be
political pressure by certain interest groups who are opposed
to day care in principal. In her study Mayer pointed out the
considerable effect Catholic opposition to day care has had
on New York's program.[17] Finally, in the past, those families most in need of day care, the poor and the black, have
not wielded sufficient political power to gain the necessary
services. However, as the percentage of women in the
labor market increases, this constraint should be eased
somewhat.

Several important political and social resources could
be utilized in implementing such a day-care system. First,
lobbyists for commercial day-care interests would almost
certainly favor instigation of such a program. The opening
of a new and potentially large market for their services
would surely be viewed as being in their best interests.
Secondly, those who have opposed government-operated day
care because of its "un-American, commune quality" may
be willing to accept a system based on the free enterprise
motif. Third, those in the government who have previously
opposed state financed, universal day-care plans because of
their costs may accept a voucher system in hopes of avoiding a more radical plan at some later date. Most political
observers agree with Steiner[18] that the 1970's will almost
certainly see major policy innovations in the field of public
child care programs. The voucher system may be the most
acceptable to fiscal conservatives. Fourth, in recent years
many individuals with teaching degrees have been unable to
find employment in the educational system. These excess
numbers of teachers could be effectively utilized in this day-
care system. Finally, women's interest groups such as the
National Organization of Women, the National Council of
Jewish Women and many others are continuing to place pressure on the government to develop day-care facilities. These
groups would be important and necessary allies of any proposed day care plan.

The Voucher Day Care System

Although it would be desirable, it does not appear
likely that a comprehensive child care program on a social
utility basis is politically feasible at this time. Therefore,

THE VOUCHER DAY-CARE SYSTEM

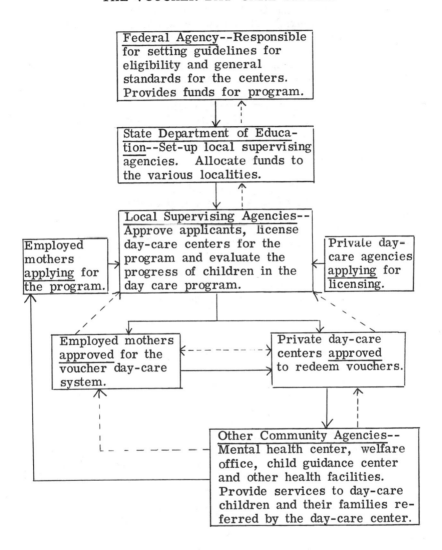

Federal Agency--Responsible for setting guidelines for eligibility and general standards for the centers. Provides funds for program.

State Department of Education--Set-up local supervising agencies. Allocate funds to the various localities.

Local Supervising Agencies-- Approve applicants, license day-care centers for the program and evaluate the progress of children in the day care program.

Employed mothers applying for the program.

Private day-care agencies applying for licensing.

Employed mothers approved for the voucher day-care system.

Private day-care centers approved to redeem vouchers.

Other Community Agencies-- Mental health center, welfare office, child guidance center and other health facilities. Provide services to day-care children and their families referred by the day-care center.

Dotted line indicates feedback

it is contended that the implementation of a day-care system might best accommodate that group most in need of services --employed mothers. This system would have the following characteristics:

1. All funding for the program would come from the federal government to insure the participation of all states. These funds would be utilized to provide vouchers to working mothers on a need basis, which could be redeemed at any approved private day-care facility. The money would be allocated to the states on the basis of the number of working mothers within each state who have children between infancy and fourteen years of age.

2. The federal government would be responsible for setting the guidelines as to who would qualify for these vouchers and in what amount. This determination would be made on the basis of family income and size, and the hours of day-care service required. However, these guidelines would be flexible enough to allow for local variation in the cost of day care and the needs of the community served. The federal government would also be responsible for setting minimum standards required of day-care centers redeeming these vouchers.

3. Since this day-care system would have a strong educational component, funds for the program would be administered on the state level by the state department of education. Administration by this department would also be useful if and when day care moves into the social utility area.

4. These state offices of education would authorize the development of local agencies to administer the program on the community level. These local agencies would be responsible for licensing and approving private day-care facilities on the basis of the federal guidelines. They would also approve applicants for the voucher program. Staff for these agencies would be composed of education, health and social service specialists.

5. Finally, day-care centers redeeming these vouchers could be either private profit or non-profit organizations. They would be required to offer the following services:

a. An educationally-oriented day-care program having a specified staff-child ratio.

b. Health facilities and health care such as immunizations, preventive care and dietary supplements.

c. Opportunities for both indoor and outdoor recreational experiences.

d. Social work consultation with both parents and
their children. This social work service would
function as a referral source to other community
agencies.

e. Transportation service to and from the center
where necessary.

f. Open to all children between infancy and fourteen years of age on a nondiscriminatory basis.

Priorities in Activating the System

Priority in activating this system would be given to
those applicants with children under six who have the lowest
incomes. This temporary measure would have to be taken
to allow the number of available day-care centers to catch
up with this larger market. Although such a priority would
not guarantee service to the greatest number of children for
the lowest cost, it would reach that group most in need of
day-care service.

Evaluation Criteria and the Feedback Subsystem

Effectiveness of this program will be measured in
terms of the system's stated objectives. This evaluation
will be conducted by administering standardized tests to random samples of those children receiving day-care services
through the system. These tests will be administered on a
longitudinal basis and will measure the educational, health
and social development of the children served, in comparison to control groups not in the day-care system. Necessary changes within the system will be accomplished by
alterations or additions to the standards required of participating day-care centers.

Another function of the evaluation process will be to
determine any possible "spillover effects" of the day-care

system.   Such a large new program is almost certain to affect those systems interacting with it.   For instance, if the
day-care centers do succeed in better preparation of children
for entry into the school system, this may have certain consequences in relation to the curriculum offered by the school
system.   It is possible that the children who have been in
day care may be ready for a more advanced program than
the school system is prepared to offer.   Also, if this day-
care system were highly successful in meeting its objectives, another possible spillover effect might be that the
system will become obsolete.   As parents who are ineligible
for the services of this system become aware of its success, they would almost certainly press for the expansion of
the system.   This impetus could quite possibly result in the
provision of day care on a social utility basis for all in
need of it.

Notes

1.   See Leonard Goodwin, A Study of the Work Orientations
     of Welfare Recipients.   Brookings Institution (Wash-
     ington, D. C. , 1971).

2.   Alfred Kadushin, Child Welfare Services.   (New York:
     The Macmillan Company, 1967), p. 318.

3.   Ibid. , p. 34.

4.   Gilbert Y. Steiner, "Child Care: New Social Policy
     Battleground, " The Brookings Bulletin, IX, No. 1
     (1972), p. 6-9.

5.   Eleanor Hart, "Day Care Centers Needed 'Desperately, '
     Report Says, " Miami Herald, April 9, 1972.

6.   Anna B. Mayer, "Day Care as a Social Instrument: A
     Policy Paper, " School of Social Work, Columbia
     University, 1965, p. 7, citing Facts About Children,
     Children's Bureau, U. S. Department of Health, Edu-
     cation and Welfare, 1962.

7.   Kadushin, op. cit. , p. 316.

8.   Ibid. , p. 317.

9.   Anna B. Mayer, "Day Care as a Social Instrument: A

Policy Paper, " School of Social Work, Columbia University, 1965, p. 7, citing Working Mothers and Day Care Services in the United States, Children's Bureau, U. S. Department of Health, Education and Welfare, 1962.

10. Anna B. Mayer, "Day Care as a Social Instrument: A Policy Paper, " School of Social Work, Columbia University, 1965, p. 26-27.

11. Ibid. , p. 98.

12. S. Res. 530, 92d Cong. , 1st sess. (1971).

13. Steiner, op. cit.

14. Ibid.

15. Alice M. Rivlin, Systematic Thinking for Social Action. (Washington: The Brookings Institution, 1972), p. 137.

16. Anna B. Mayer, "Day Care as a Social Instrument: A Policy Paper, " School of Social Work, Columbia University, 1965, p. 49, citing Facts About Children, Children's Bureau, U. S. Department of Health, Education and Welfare, 1962.

17. Anna B. Mayer, "Day Care as a Social Instrument: A Policy Paper, " School of Social Work, Columbia University, 1965, p. 128-31.

18. Steiner, op. cit.

Bibliography

Evans, E. Belle, Beth Shub, and Marlene Weinstein. Day Care. United States: Beacon Press, 1971.

Hart, Eleanor. "Day Care Centers Needed 'Desperately, ' Report Says, " Miami Herald, April 9, 1972.

Kadushin, Alfred. Child Welfare Services. New York: The Macmillan Company, 1967.

Marcussen, Clifford C. , "Learn, Baby, Learn, " The Plain

Truth, XXXVII (March-April, 1972), p. 23-28.

Mayer, Anna B. "Day Care as a Social Instrument: A
Policy Paper." School of Social Work, Columbia University, 1965.

Rivlin, Alice M. Systematic Thinking for Social Action.
Washington: The Brookings Institute, 1971.

Ruderman, Florence A. Child Care and Working Mothers.
New York: Child Welfare League of America, Inc.,
1968.

Steiner, Gilbert Y. "Child Care: New Social Policy Battle-
ground," The Brookings Bulletin, IX (Winter, 1972),
p. 6-9.

13. THE HELPING SERVICES IN A LIMITED GROWTH, SERVICE-ORIENTED SOCIETY

An affluent society develops a demand for increased services, including social welfare services. A mature society in a community of nations tends to become interested in economy and efficiency because rapid growth no longer provides an effective cover for inefficiency. The United States may be viewed as a near-mature society in a community of nations with travel and communication equipment which render isolation impossible. We have a proclivity toward trying to solve simple problems which immediately confront us, whereas intervention at a higher level in the social systems hierarchy might prevent the occurrence of many of these pressing problems. Despite the attractiveness of immediate problems, which sometimes stimulate interest because of tittilating attributes, our society is experiencing the negatives of such growing problems as pollution and population growth.

The Black Scenario

The Club of Rome studies which considered interdependent economic, political, natural, and social components have brought attention to a world community stake in cooperative efforts to enhance and maintain more widely distributed standards for an acceptable quality of life. The inhumane and, possibly, non-utilitarian policy of maintaining rates of economic growth in affluent countries while millions of people in underdeveloped countries are suffering is being questioned. In discussing this predicament of mankind, Darella Meadows and others reached the following conclusion concerning growth rates, their tradeoff costs, and the worldwide impact on the quality of life.

> They demonstrate that the process of economic growth, as it is occurring today, is inexorably widening the gap between the rich and the poor nations of the world.[1]

179

Since the decline in some aspects of the quality of
life, such as pollution, appear to be directly related to economic growth, affluent nations have been able to limit deteri-
oration of the environment at the expense of backward countries. Consequently, we have experienced positive feedback
which has encouraged continued economic growth, but the
Club of Rome reports indicate that we are now experiencing
an induced negative feedback which will serve to reduce both
economic growth and the quality of life. Worldwide thermo-
static type controls are defined as being operative to the extent of causing a catastrophic turn-around. The Club of
Rome conclusions are:

1. Under present growth trends, even with our current environmental dividend related to the misery of underdeveloped countries, the growth limit in the world environment will be reached within a hundred years. Existing
trends in world population, industrialization, pollution, food
production, and resource depletion will probably result in a
sudden and dramatic decline in population and industrial
capacity.

2. However, it is possible through planning and controls to produce conditions of ecological and economic stability that could continue far into the future.

3. The time to start vigorous policy determination
and planning is now. [2]

Economists recognize the existence of the problems
mentioned by the doomsday prophets but they question the
probability of catastrophe and/or the necessity of the government to intervene through strict controls to prevent disaster. They maintain that industry and other systems will
respond to quality of life demands and that encouraging trends
are already in evidence; but a spokesman for business and
economics, Tilford Gaines, Senior Vice President and Economist for Manufacturer's Hanover Trust, concludes:

> This sketchy analysis of the hopeful evidence in
> the American economy is in no way intended to be
> a rebuttal of the work that has been done by a
> number of ecologists and other scholars and, most
> particularly of the conclusions derived from the
> model recently devised at MIT under the sponsor-
> ship of The Club of Rome. The concern on the
> future of life on earth shared by so many scientists

certainly demands that the issues be treated seriously. With that in mind, it is critically important that the MIT group make the full details of its model and of its statistical input broadly available to independent groups of social and physical scientists in order that the validity of the assumptions and of the findings may be appraised. [3]

Some Supplementary Predictions for the United States

If we are to move to a world of service and de-emphasize production of goods, under conditions of limited growth because we have reached a static optimum or because of catastrophes envisaged by the Club of Rome reports, there are significant effects on manpower needs and roles of significance to social work and other helping services. Denis F. Johnston has projected three additional scenarios.

1. The Green Scenario advanced by Charles A. Reich[4] and others, which foresees widespread displacement of workers at all levels--blue collar, white collar and service--with most "work" being performed by an elite of highly trained cybernetic experts, and the majority of people facing the challenge of how to maximize as consumers in the "green society" rather than being concerned with problems of productivity. This vision is similar to that of William Godwin and the elder Malthus in the eighteenth century.

2. The Blue Scenario predicts a full employment economy which will develop policies to remove the barriers to employment. This scenario assumes that the pace and focus of technological change is altered so as to sustain a high level of demand for workers, and so that there will be an adequate supply of properly trained people who want to work. This viewpoint assumes: (a) that automation will continue to expand the number and variety of professional, technical, and service jobs essential to technological change; (b) that there will be shifts to labor-intensive work designed to reduce the social costs of our current patterns of production; (c) that we will accept the challenge cf helping backward countries increase production and income, so generating demand for labor in the United States; and (d) that the Protestant Ethic will retain its health and vigor. Faith would remain with market forces as a maximizer of human welfare.

But a segment of the Blue Scenario group sees increased necessity for centralized governmental planning. Government is viewed as the employer of first, not last resort. The contention is that solutions to pressing social and economic problems can emerge only through government initiative and coordination.

3. The Turquoise Scenario assumes continued improvement through technological change geared to the needs of human beings, but maintains that economic security and wealth accumulation through a growing cybernetic technology carry with them a demand for efficient workers in four major areas:

(1) a core of highly trained technicians and engineers needed to maintain and improve machinery of production and distribution, supplemented by a growing corps of ombudsmen to provide the feedback information needed to direct this machinery in accordance with public wishes and agreed-upon social values; (2) a growing number of workers in the fields of public and personal services; (3) a growing number of craftsmen and artisans whose handiwork continues to be valued because of its individualistic, nonmachine characteristics and stylistic qualities; and (4) a major expansion of employment in what Toffler has aptly termed the experience industries--a blending of recreational and educational opportunities packaged to appeal to the interests of an increasingly affluent and educated population enjoying greater amounts of leisure time. [5]

Implications for the Social Sciences and Helping Services

The uncertainties of the future make for indecision about social work and other helping service educational policies. But there is a thread which suggests the need for more effective social science input through all of the scenario predictions. Even under the "Green Scenario" there is a need for some highly trained elitist policy makers and planners using sophisticated science and social science tools, even though most need only to learn how to consume with "gusto" and enjoy the good life. But, if the other scenarios are more likely, and current evidence would suggest that they are, then there will be a great impact of highly-trained applied social scientists as the social changes demand effectiveness in such roles. More effective information retrieval and use in the social sciences will be needed to effect the emergence of a Rose Scenario.

A Model for Achieving More Effective Use of Social Science

As the Club of Rome project utilized cybernetic techniques to make their predictions--and none of the scenarios neglected the growing importance of cybernetics (the understanding and control of systems)--an effective approach to instituting improved information retrieval must likewise consider a systemic approach employing computer technology. The term "model" refers to an approach, utilizing system analysis, that considers a set of components which are satisfactorily bounded and interrelated to achieve efficiency (full use of delegated inputs) and effectiveness (results which adequately satisfy stated objectives).

Normative forecasting, an essential ingredient of effective social welfare planning and helping service education, requires scientific systems analysis as a prerequisite for prediction. The following format is adaptable to a variety of problem-solving situations in which forecasting is an essential part.

The Information Retrieval Problem

There is a long-standing and growing accumulation of evidence that the transfer of knowledge from the social sciences into practice has not been sufficiently effective in the development of viable strategies for problem prevention and for the restoration of impaired client functioning. Part of this lag has been the result of focusing on the re-education of the client toward a goal of satisfactory functioning as defined by our social values, e.g., the Protestant Ethic, in the face of massive social systems constraints. But a very large part of the problem has been the inability to help service instructors and their output, practitioners, to use available scientific knowledge effectively. In assessing the problem, Martin Bloom concluded:

> Compared to what the social worker needs to know about the structure, function, and development of individuals, groups, and societies, the amount of

truly usable scientific knowledge is very inadequate.
This is a crisis of poverty of usable knowledge. 6

History of Problem Development and Analysis

Bloom's conclusion was preceded by a growing concern among a number of leading social work educators, including Coyle (1952 and 1958), Boehm (1951), Maas (1950),
Pollak (1951, 1952, and 1956), Greenwood (1955), Kahn-
Kadushin (1959), Stein (1955 and 1958), Warren (1967), and
Gyarfas (1969) (see Chapter II for greater detail and references). And then, after some inattention in the 1960s, concern increased as educators gained more complete realization of the ineffectiveness of direct practice models as solutions to client problems in a milieu of complex, poorly coordinated welfare systems. The interest in social systems
and planning brought a need for increased usage of social
science theory, and empirical information became more pronounced. A scanning of the literature reveals the following
barriers to effective information retrieval and conversion
into practice usage.

1. Communication--lack of agreement as to the ex-
    plication of concepts in both social sciences and
    social work.
2. Difficulties in reducing theory to workable prac-
    tice concepts.
3. Ethical and professional conflicts over research
    as a means of effecting personal and social
    change.
4. Status-related hostility between social workers
    and social scientists.
5. Conflicts over the seeking of knowledge for prob-
    lem-solving versus knowledge for the sake of
    truth as an end.
6. The obvious time lag between theory generation
    and conversion to application to practice prob-
    lems.
7. Professional chauvinism.
8. The personality system bias of the clinical or
    medical model.

More careful observation of the problem suggests that
there are systemic failures which may prove to be correct-
able despite the historic constraints listed above. It is possible that students could be required to take more basic

social science, that instructors be required to get more
graduate training in social science, or that systems for stor-
ing, retrieving, and tailoring information for the needs and
demands of users could be improved. Figure 1 shows how
social science-social work interrelationships have tended to
become a dead-end Black Hole of Calcutta, rather than a
little understood but effective Black Box for the informal
transfer of social science knowledge to social work practice.

Weaknesses are mutual, but perhaps the social worker has the greater problem in theory application. When a
social scientist conducting research wants to connect theory
with reality, he has a body of principles derived from science to guide his efforts. Social work has recognized this
need, but professionals are just in the process of devising
sufficient and efficient guidelines for this purpose. Admittedly, inputs from social science could be improved if social
indicators were further developed so that consequences of
social change could be more accurately forecast to enable
more effective strategy recommendations. Also, improvements in social work knowledge and a more comprehensive
definition of practice roles as related to social change would
improve the input effectiveness of practitioners. But the
need for a more effective retrieval, filtering, and synthesis
of social science knowledge is indicated. Perhaps there is
a need for movement from an informal, poorly defined means
of information interchange to a more satisfactorily bounded
and functionally interrelated information sub-system.

As the demand has increased for efficient performance
of worker roles, in addition to inputs toward direct behavior
changing, so has the awareness that social science input is
insufficient to insure effective performance of additional
roles. Examples of these roles (previously discussed) are:
social brokerage (liaison between clients and agencies and
among agencies); advocacy (pleading intelligently for client
rights within the constraints of existing systems); or mobilization (using theory, fact, and skill to help regroup existing
social services or secure needed legislation and/or appropriate administrative changes). Also, demands by Congress,
legislatures, and the public for accountability have increased;
as has the need for knowledge of systems analysis in a social systems context. These factors serve to increase the
need for applied social science. In the social worker employment market there is negative feedback. Without regard
to the primary objective in completing the social welfare
curriculum, Florida State University student job-getting

FIGURE I

Interrelationship Problems of Utilizing Social Science in
Practicing the Client-Social Systems Practice Model

POTENTIAL SOCIAL SCIENCE INPUT

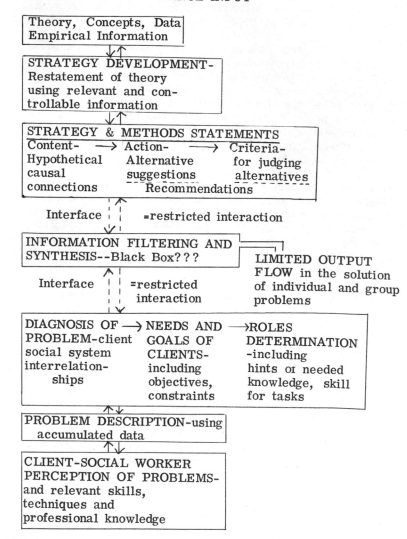

Theory, Concepts, Data
Empirical Information

STRATEGY DEVELOPMENT-
Restatement of theory
using relevant and con-
trollable information

STRATEGY & METHODS STATEMENTS
Content- ⟶ Action- ⟶ Criteria-
Hypothetical   Alternative   for judging
causal   suggestions   alternatives
connections   Recommendations

Interface   =restricted interaction

INFORMATION FILTERING AND
SYNTHESIS--Black Box???

LIMITED OUTPUT
FLOW in the solution
of individual and group
problems

Interface   =restricted
                interaction

DIAGNOSIS OF ⟶ NEEDS AND ⟶ROLES
PROBLEM-client   GOALS OF   DETERMINATION
social system   CLIENTS-   -including
interrelation-   including   hints of needed
ships   objectives,   knowledge, skill
                 constraints   for tasks

PROBLEM DESCRIPTION-using
accumulated data

CLIENT-SOCIAL WORKER
PERCEPTION OF PROBLEMS-
and relevant skills,
techniques and
professional knowledge

SOCIAL WORK INSTRUCTOR KNOWLEDGE INPUTS

success in social work was as follows: 1966--68%; 1967--
62%; 1968--56%; 1969--48%; 1970--35%; and 1971--31%.
Grant requests require a systems format and, if requests
concern problems of delivering effective social services,
then social science knowledge is needed to define the problem and to carry out research or pilot projects effectively
and with research evaluation, if the grant is to gain favorable funding action.

Tradeoff Pressures of the Current Educational Environment

The need for a more effective information retrieval
and utilization system is further indicated by the growing
competition for teacher and student time, to the extent that
lengthy assignments for students and heavy teacher investment in library time are becoming increasingly difficult.
Value conflicts relate to the following tradeoffs:

1. Study vs committee participation;
2. Scholarship vs. campus political activity;
3. Scholarship vs peer group approval;
4. Scholarship vs comfort at lower levels of the
   Maslow hierarchy;
5. Scholarly output vs power acquisition;
6. Long-run recognition vs short-run response;
7. Maintenance of academic standards vs job con-
   tinuity through large class enrollments;
8. Academic reputation vs material gain through
   other means;
9. Quality control vs degree quantity output.

Problem Implications of the Existing System and Sub-systems

An effective information storage, retrieval, and utilization system should accomplish basic goals which serve a
clientele composed of: (1) instructors, (2) students, (3)
practitioners seeking improved effectiveness, and (4) policy
makers seeking information which will assist in planning for
improved social systems.   The existing information resources
are described in Figure II.

In addition to the diffuse, caveat emptor, supermarket
appearance of the existing process of information storage,
retrieval, and use by faculty and students, there are other
serious deficiencies:

FIGURE II

Existing University Information Retrieval and Use Vector Relationships

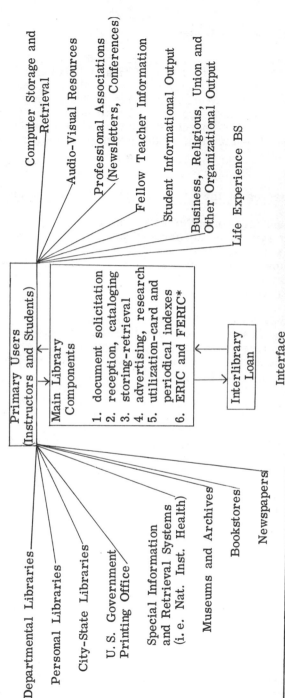

Primary Users (Instructors and Students)

Main Library Components
1. document solicitation
2. reception, cataloging
3. storing-retrieval
4. advertising, research
5. utilization-card and periodical indexes
6. ERIC and FERIC*

Interlibrary Loan

Interface

Computer Storage and Retrieval
Audio-Visual Resources
Professional Associations (Newsletters, Conferences)
Fellow Teacher Information
Student Informational Output
Business, Religious, Union and Other Organizational Output
Life Experience BS

Departmental Libraries
Personal Libraries
City-State Libraries
U. S. Government Printing Office
Special Information and Retrieval Systems (i.e. Nat. Inst. Health)
Museums and Archives
Bookstores
Newspapers

ENVIRONMENT: the parent university or college, the state system of higher education, private educational agencies, state government, elementary and secondary school systems, federal agencies, especially the Department of Health, Education and Welfare, local governments, legal restrictions on information gathering and use, time, money, values and attitudes of the general public, professional values and attitudes

*FERIC=Florida Educational Recovery Information Center; ERIC=Educational Resources Information Center

1. the systems components are not adequately inter-
    related.

2. coordination and filtering become largely a laissez
    faire and haphazard process because the challenge
    is too great for most faculty and students.

3. time and knowledge-base demands discourage us-
    age of available materials.

4. there is evidence of knowledge base deficiencies
    in social science which serve to limit usage,
    such as:

    (a) basic studies requirements which permit stu-
        dents to graduate with no or little credit in
        economics, sociology, political science, and/or
        anthropology;

    (b) social work curriculum requirements which
        require no or very limited preparation in so-
        cial science;

    (c) limited hiring of social work faculty with
        graduate concentrations other than social work
        as indicated by the Pearman-McLean study
        which found only 32 percent of undergraduate
        social work faculty with a year or more
        graduate study above the MSW and 39 percent
        with the MSW only (see Chapter III).   Onken
        (1968) reported that 60 percent of graduate
        faculties had not taken course work beyond
        the MSW and that there were only nine gradu-
        ate social work faculty members with a doc-
        torate in economics and, also, only nine with
        doctorates in political science or public ad-
        ministration in United States.[7]

    (d) data collection through the use of computer
        retrieval and storage does not insure effective
        usage.

An evaluative scheme which would aid appraisal of the
effectiveness of existing systems would be a logical step.
Figure III is suggested with the warning that the evaluations
are based on little more than observation and experience.[8]

FIGURE III
User Problem Identification Matrix for Information Retrieval and Use in a University Library

SYSTEMS FUNCTIONS	FACULTY - hrs. of grad. soc. sc.		STUDENTS - hours of soc. sc.	
	With 25 qrt. hrs.	Less than 25 hrs.	With 25 qrt. hrs.	Less than 25 qt. hrs.
Documentation solicitation and accumulation	adequate	very adequate	adequate	very adequate
Reception and Cataloging	inadequate	adequate	adequate	adequate
Storing of books and other sources	adequate	adequate	adequate	adequate
Retrievability	inadequate	very inadequate	inadequate	very inadequate
Relevance Filter				
identifiability	inadequate	very inadequate	very inadequate	very inadequate
applicability	inadequate	very inadequate	very inadequate	very inadequate
user fitting	inadequate	very inadequate	very inadequate	very inadequate
Validity guarantee	inadequate	inadequate	very inadequate	very inadequate
System control over user techniques	inadequate	inadequate	very inadequate	very inadequate
General Appraisal	inadequate	very inadequate	very inadequate	very inadequate

Very adequate - Function sufficiently strong to satisfy effectiveness criteria
Adequate = Function sufficiently strong to satisfy effectiveness criteria for most users
Inadequate = Performance somewhat below reasonable standards for effectiveness
Very inadequate = Performance far below reasonable standards for effectiveness

Surveys of user experience with reference to locating specific social science information bits could be employed to test the validity of the impressionistic appraisal contained in Figure III. Also, user attitudes and values could be determined through ranking desired attributes against rankings of existing library functions on the basis of performance standards. Time and motion studies, attribute analysis, and utilization studies might further upgrade the level of the problem identification matrix. In addition, pilot projects could be activated to test incremental attempts to improve existing information services as an alternative to more radical changes.

University and college computer-oriented systems are being used to strengthen information and use processes. An example of a recent innovation, the Florida Educational Recovery Information Center, is pictured in Figure IV.

Systems improvements such as that illustrated in Figure IV may prove to be effective in the correction of some deficiencies, but it is apparent that important needs are not being met. Some of the remaining problems which must be explored and corrected are:

1. Multiple information indexes require checking many retrieval tools, e.g., ERIC, several periodical and dissertation indexes, Sociological Abstracts, Social Work Abstracts, Poverty and Human Resources Abstracts. ERIC centralizes social science abstracting at the University of Colorado. Coverage is not complete and some abstracts provide very little information.

2. Time and knowledge limitations restrict efficient use of existing systems.

3. Categories frequently do not break from the general to intermediate and on down to specific references in some areas of applied social science, e.g., systems relationships. In information science terminology, descriptor classifications are not adequate to meet user demands.

4. Existing services provide a limited quality and relevance filter. The Query I system used by FERIC does not service the established descriptor term, "relevance."

5. Inadequate user image determination limits systems effectiveness.

FIGURE IV

The FERIC System

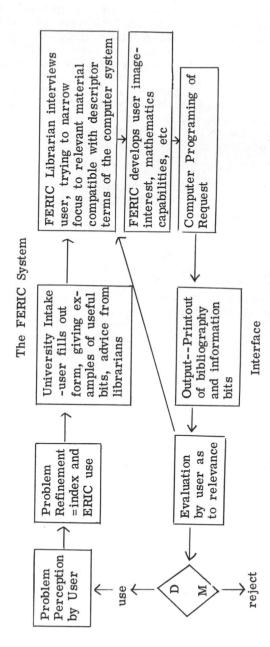

ENVIRONMENT--the university, the State Department of Education, laws concerning the obtaining and use of information

6. School and departmental systemization of information retrieval and usage is largely lacking.

Systems analysis as related to information retrieval should explore strengths and weakness of current sub-systems with the central goal of discovering improved or new means of insuring more effective use of social science information. Figure V provides a format for further investigation of problems and the development of criteria for the comparison of possible solutions to these problems. Criteria should provide tools for the efficient evaluation of existing, revised, or new information retrieval sub-systems in relation to specific program objectives. Full consideration should be given to existing potential resources and restraints.

FIGURE V

Format for the Development of a Viable Information
Retrieval and Utilization System

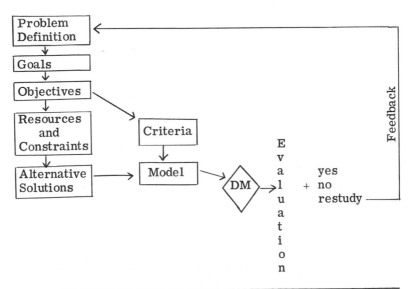

Environment: the university, other universities, colleges
              and junior colleges, state government, federal
              government, parents, taxpayers

Goal Formulation

Problem definition has been treated in depth. Determination of the nature of the social science information retrieval problem, including discovery of attributes of existing systems, is a basic step in systems analysis. An important phase of the problem which was discussed is the diversity and inconsistency of the values of potential users of systems of social science retrieval for helping service practice. Goals must be related to values in order to develop an effective system. Planners must expect barriers related to value conflicts of potential users of information systems. Some general theory such as an application of Maslow's hierarchy of values from meeting physical needs to self-actualization may be applied, but specific theory development related to more specific values of social science retrieval system users is in the infant stage. In a discussion of this matter, Suzanne Y. Felton, an information scientist for Smith, Kline and French of Philadelphia, states:

> Research on communications in the behavioral sciences indicates that there may be values and attitudes toward behavioral science information that are similar to those in science. However, the work is presently rather inconclusive....
>
> To summarize, then, the sociology of information has not been widely or adequately researched. At its best, as with science information, it is spotty and peripheral to other studies. At its worst, as with the humanities, it has been almost nonexistent. [9] (Felton, as judged from the text of the article, appeared to be using the behavioral science term in its broader usage which includes social sciences.)

The limited knowledge of predominant values of theoretical and applied social scientists makes the fitting of information retrieval systems to users difficult. At the initial stage, empirical information produced through an ordinal ranking of user value choices could provide helpful guidelines in setting goals and objectives. In light of the existing state of knowledge concerning values, the hierarchy of goals listed below is tentative.

Goal I: To increase the effective use of social science information in social work and related helping service practice.

Measurable Objectives:

1. To reduce appreciably the time necessary to obtain relevant social science information in harmony with a quantitative measure established through testing user expectations.

2. To increase the amount of social science used, as measured by increases in the number of social science disciplines utilized and the depth of conceptual knowledge of each subject matter area.

3. To decrease the time lag between the generation of new social science theory, facts, and related technological innovations and their practice application.

Goal II: To improve instructional techniques and processes.

Measurable Objectives:

1. To increase the use of social science information retrieval sources by faculty and students.

2. To raise the level of relevance of information supplied by retrieval systems to the problem need of users.

3. To raise the level of Gestalt perception of instructors. (Observational teams of specialists could determine whether information was being used in partial or erroneous ways or with complete conceptual understanding.)

Goal III: To encourage the arrangement of education structures for the optimal usage of social science information by the helping services.

Measurable Objective:

1. To accomplish restructuring which encourages cooperation between empirical and theoretical social scientists and the helping professions, e.g., a school of applied social science or a generalist-specialist information retrieval team.

Goal IV: To present proposals in a format which facilitates cost-effectiveness or cost-benefit analysis.

Measurable Objectives:

1.   To derive models which will set acceptable standards and consider alternatives which meet these standards with the least direct and indirect costs.

2.   To develop means for measuring costs and benefits over time in dollar terms and permit ranking alternatives ordinally by cost-benefit ratios.

Goal V: To originate alternatives which are within budgetary possibilities.

Measurable Objective:

1.   To develop alternatives which are: (a) within limitations of current budgerary allotments; (b) within limitations of current allowances plus possible transfers of unencumbered funds; or (c) within probabilities of potential appropriations.

Goal VI: To improve the competitive position of helping service graduates vis-a-vis college graduates in general in securing helping service employment.

Measurable Objectives:

1.   To raise the level of scoring in comprehensive tests such as the Graduate Record Examination and civil service tests.

2.   To increase the hiring rate of graduates in social work and other helping service professions.

3.   To improve the level of solicited agency evaluations of alumni performance during the early months of employment and at later intervals.

Goal VII: To improve user attitude toward retrieval systems.

Measurable Objective:

1.   To increase positive responses as compared to the levels of initial evaluative surveys.

Criteria

Criteria should provide concrete measures of objective and goal fulfillment. Corresponding with the goals listed above, logical criteria would be:

1a. What is the time required to find and incorporate needed information?

1b. What is the extent of social science usage in relation to an established time base?

2a. What is the frequency of the use of information retrieval systems with reference to an established pre-innovation time base?

2b. What is the degree of relevance of information system references as compared to the time base?

2c. What is the level of understanding of social science as shown by faculty and student performance with reference to the time base?

3. What facilitating structures will best serve to accomplish functional objectives?

4. What evaluation model or models will most efficiently compare alternative systems?

5. Is the alternative within the range of budgetary possibilities?

6. As to time and competitor comparisons, have graduates improved their position in the job market?

7. Do users "like" the system?

The potential for using the suggested criteria for the measurement of success in meeting standards set for objective satisfaction is limited by the complexities of cause and effect. It is possible that improvement may occur because of increased motivation from the environment, e. g., the knowledge that civil service examinations were including more social science-related questions in helping services examinations. Also, a change in policies within the instructional system, such as stronger admissions requirements as to social science knowledge, might be the real cause of change revealed through the listed criteria rather than information system improvements per se. In so far as possible, such externalities should be measured.

Resources and Constraints

There are many actual and potential resources for improving information retrieval and usage systems on college and university campuses. Among the possibilities are: (1) instructional improvement grants; (2) released time for participating professors; (3) budget flexibility or special state and/or federal grants for improving information systems; (4) the accumulated knowledge of faculty and students; and (5) specialist facilities and specialist personnel, such as libraries and librarians, computer centers and computer programmers.

Constraints are also numerous. C. West Churchman, in an abstract of a paper on operations research prospects for libraries, stated:

> Operations research can be described in terms of a specific strategy of research. The purpose of this paper is to describe and criticize a very common strategy in which the operations researcher relies strongly on managerial judgment and the existing system as a basis for his inquiry. In this strategy, the operations researcher takes the libraries and specifically user behavior as givens and relies heavily on library administration as a basis for his models and his data. The current strategy is criticized in idealistic terms. It may well be that operations researchers are solving the wrong problems because the existing system-- for example, the library--may be seriously faulty in its design with respect to real clients. 10

In support of Churchman's contention, our request from the FERIC computerized information retrieval system, which was handled with minimal delay, produced ten pounds of output and 1,109 bibliographic listings, with about 1,000 containing bit abstracts. In response to a request for copies of what appeared to be the most important reference, The Journal of the American Society for Information Science, a large university user of FERIC had no listing in the master periodical file indicating that the library had this periodical and that it could be found in a special library for librarians.

In summary, constraints may include personal habits, the quality of information service available, the speed and costs of services available, operations policies of information agencies, and regulatory controls placed on literature and data.

There are at least two aspects of controls and/or

selective emphasis on the production of literature and data
which merit attention:

1.   A perusal of the FERIC output on information retrieval produced the conclusion that very little has been
done relative to tailoring the system for social science operations.   The two beginning efforts which were discovered
were "a machine readable data base of social science serials, " and "Urbandoc, " which aims to improve bibliographic
services for the urban affairs specialist with special attention to social science information.[11]

2.   Accrediting and professional membership organizations may provide barriers to the effective bridging of
social science information into effective practitioner usage
through one or more of the following practices.
        a.   Overriding their general statements concern-
ing the importance of applied social science by approving
educational curricula which require little or no social science.
        b.   Specific personnel requirements which ignore
or severely restrict faculty recruitment emphasizing graduate preparation in the social sciences.
        c.   Narrow selectivity of papers for publication
in house journals or for delivery at national meetings of organizations.   The utilization of social science information
may have a low priority.

Such a "dirty filter" effect may actually discourage
instructors from exerting additional effort to learn and use
more social science information or from showing interest in
new innovations which might reduce the time and effort necessary for more effective use of social science.

Data Collection and Evaluation

Systems may be evaluated at several levels of system
and sub-system operation.   Efficiency evaluation entails
monitoring to see if the planned inputs are being made.
Effectiveness measures concern system outputs at various
levels.   In assessing the effectiveness of an information systems change, data on performance, changes in relevant external variables, and impact on sub-system relationships
can be accumulated.   To some extent, the TOTE system of
monitoring may be applied.   Incremental changes may be
made and continued if system operation improves, or can be

dropped if the impact is judged to be negative. The components of the system may be checked by comparing alternative inputs. For example, the filter, intake, or receiver-processor function may be tested by using personnel with alternative qualifications. One research effort found technical feedback between filter personnel and the user to be important, but little difference in whether a highly-trained biological scientist or a receptionist was utilized in this role. 12 Experience of others may be utilized in developing cost-effectiveness appraisals of new social science information systems. Donald W. King and Peggy W. Neel of Westat Research Incorporated illustrate this in the following abstract included in the FERIC output.

> A recently developed cost-effectiveness model for on-line retrieval systems is discussed through use of an example utilizing performance results collected from several independent sources and cost data derived for a recently completed study of the American Psychological Association. One of the primary attributes of this model rests in its great flexibility, in that various combinations of alternative systems and subsystems are open to comparison. Some of the systems which have been addressed include batch processing, and on-line abstracts and the subsystems include various levels of recall, several types of screening, and different user systems interfaces. 13

Simulation and testing of selective changes may be used to pre-test alternatives among possible systems changes. 14 In some instances, cost-benefit analysis may be employed under the following or a similar formula. To what extent is

$$\frac{b1}{(1+i)^1} + \frac{b2}{(1+i)^2} + \frac{b3}{(1+i)^3} \cdots \cdots \frac{bn + s}{(1+i)n}$$

$$> \frac{c1}{(1+i)^1} + \frac{c2}{(1+i)^2} + \frac{c3}{(1+i)^3} \cdots \cdots \frac{cn}{(1+i)n}$$

when b1, b2, b3....bn are a series of expected benefits over time
c1, c2, c3.... cn are a series of anticipated costs over time
s = scrap recovery value
i is the appropriate rate of discount for compounding over time[15]

Feedback obtained from surveys of users, former students, agency supervisors, and graduate school representatives may also be used in evaluation. Operation research specialists could be employed to evaluate the effectiveness of the system. [16]

Alternatives

Alternatives can be generated from the evaluative outputs mentioned in the preceding discussion of data collection and evaluation. The systems analyst's rule-of-thumb is to intervene at the highest possible level of effectiveness. This strategy removes some of the problem of judging the impact of troublesome variables which lie outside of the defined system boundaries. Also, there is the likelihood that cost-benefit relations can be improved through this strategy. Some suggested alternatives for improving social science utilization are

1. Raising the basic level of student and faculty receptivity by requiring increased preparation in the social sciences.
2. Creation of an information retrieval team composed of social scientists, helping service instructors, information specialists, and students. Some gains might be made from the interchange of personal knowledge, arriving at common definitions of key terms, and in obtaining leads for the improvement and use of higher level information systems.
3. Improvement in the functioning of existing information retrieval systems, especially as to their capacity to serve social scientists.
4. Some combination of 1, 2 and 3.
5. Creation of a predominantly new system.
6. Maintenance of the status quo.

There is considerable complexity involved in the planning and implementation of computerized information systems, as suggested by Elizabeth Fong in her summary of progress in this effort:

> In addition to reviewing the characteristics of document processing systems, this paper pays considerable attention to the description of a system via a feature list approach. The purpose of this

report is to present features of the systems in
parallel fashion to facilitate comparison so that
the potential user may have a basis for evaluation
in terms of the capacities which his requirements
demand. The state-of-the-art in on-line document
processing systems has been moving very rapidly.
The software progress in data base management,
heuristic programming, automatic abstracting and
indexing and, also, the hardware progress in front-
end computers, optical character recognition devices, on-line data entry devices, etc., all have
played a part. [17]

Model for Solution Determination

If the heuristic approach to improving information retrieval systems (described and summarized in Figure V) becomes activated, then there must be some scheme for making a choice among the alternatives which have been suggested. At the point of applying the model suggested in Figure VI, all of the steps in Figure V should be reviewed to
determine whether or not all relevant viewpoints are being
considered at each step in the process. Criteria for the
success of a study should include not only whether a plan is
accepted by a decision maker, but also, whether or not it
is implemented and, later, if implemented, whether feedback
suggests the improvements called for in the program objectives. This is to say that the planning process should include efficiency monitoring and evaluation of effectiveness.
An appropriate cost-effectiveness model would minimize
costs in relation to standards; the end step would be the sub-
mission of the evaluative report to concerned administrators
and decision makers.

Anticipated Spillover Output

The Federal educational amendments of 1972 (P. L.
92-318) Title III, Section 405 provided for the establishment
of a National Institute of Education at the same level as the
HEW Office of Education, responsible to a newly designated
Assistant Secretary for Education. ERIC has been transferred to NIE and it is possible that educational research,
and especially that concerning information systems, will be
upgraded. A university based information improvement project, regardless of final solution, could:

FIGURE VI

Model to be Used in Considering Alternative Problem Solutions

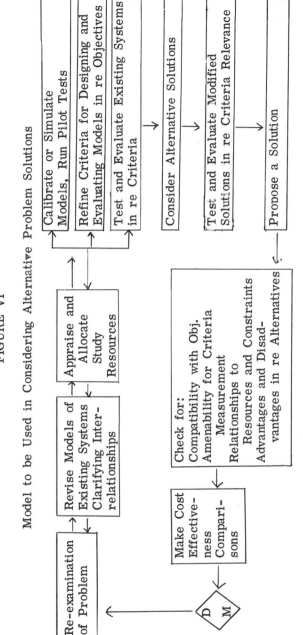

1. Provide a state of readiness for utilizing new Federal resources.
2. Increase the usage of existing state and university systems.
3. Improve the dialogue between social scientists and helping service specialists, thus raising communications effectiveness.
4. Provide feedback for existing information systems, thereby providing input for evaluation and possible improvements.

Postscript

This book is dedicated to the purpose of establishing the importance of social science in social work and other helping professions in a period of crisis. President Nixon strives for greater control and cost-effectiveness at the federal level. His second-term cabinet appointments reflect this purpose, especially as regards the Department of Health, Education and Welfare. States are being threatened with losses of federal matching money because of failure satisfactorily to implement accountability guidelines. These external and internal political pressures have caused the states to struggle for higher levels of cost-effectiveness in the administration of income maintenance and helping service programs. A functionally illiterate high school student is suing the educational system in California because of the state's failure to prepare him for a job. Education at all levels is being challenged because of inadequate accountability. Both clients and the public are questioning the social welfare system through political and legal actions. The systems format is being emphasized in defining problems and seeking viable solutions. Social science has a central role in this campaign.

Notes

1. Donella Meadows, et al., The Limits To Growth (New York: Universe Books for Potomac Associates, 1972), pp. 43-44.

2. Ibid., for a more complete discussion, pp. 9-197; and Richard M. Koff, "An End to All of This," Playboy (July, 1971), pp. 206-209.

3.   Tilford Gaines, "The Doomsday Debate," Economic Report: Manufacturers Hanover Trust Company (March, 1972), unpaged leaflet.

4.   Charles Reich, The Greening of America (New York: Random House, 1970).

5.   See Denis F. Johnston, "The Future of Work: Three Possible Alternatives," Monthly Labor Review (May, 1972), pp. 5-6 and pp. 3-10 for a more complete discussion of the three scenarios. Further understanding can be obtained by reading Alvin Toffler, Future Shock (New York: Random House, Bantam edition, 1970).

6.   Martin Bloom, "The Selection of Knowledge from the Behavioral Sciences and its Integration into Social Work Curricula," Journal of Education for Social Work, 5 (Spring, 1969), p. 16.

7.   Gerald Onken, A Survey of Faculty in Graduate Schools of Social Work (New York: Council on Social Work Education, 1968), p. 25.

8.   See C. West Churchman, The Systems Approach (New York: Dell Publishing Company, 1968), pp. 104-110 for some of the basic ideas incorporated in this chart.

9.   Suzanne Y. Felton, "Attitudes and Values Associated with Information," Drexel Library Quarterly, 7 (January, 1971).

10. See C. West Churchman, "Operations Research Prospects for Libraries: The Realities and Ideals," The Library Quarterly, 42 (January, 1972), pp. 6-14.

11. Details on these projects can be obtained through reports issued by Stephen A. Roberts, "A Machine Readable Data Base of Social Science Serials," Bath, England, University of Technology, 1971; and Dr. Vivian S. Sessions, "Urbandoc: A Bibliographic Information System Demonstration Report," Center for the Advancement of Library Information Sciences, City University of New York, 1971.

12.   See Robert G. Kincade, Science Information Require-
      ments of Scientists: The Need for a Scientific Re-
      quest Receiver and Processor in an Information
      Clearinghouse, American Institute for Research,
      Silver Springs, Maryland, 1967.

13.   Donald W. King and Peggy W. Neel, Cost Effectiveness
      of On-Line Retrieval Systems, Westat Research In-
      corporated, Rockville, Maryland.

14.   See Michael David Cooper, Evaluation of Information
      Retrieval Systems: A Simulation and Cost Approach,
      University of California, Berkeley, School of Li-
      brarianship, 1971.

15.   See George Chadwick, A Systems View of Planning (Ox-
      ford, New York: Pergamon Press, 1971), pp. 258-
      271.

16.   See Tony Tripodi, Phillip Fellin, and Irwin Epstein,
      Social Program Evaluation (Itasca, Illinois: Peacock
      Publishers, Incorporated, 1971).

17.   Elizabeth Fong, A Survey of Selected Document Pro-
      cessing Systems, Superintendent of Documents, U. S.
      Government Printing Office, Washington, D. C.,
      1971.

INDEX

Accountability 55; demand for 4,
16, 61, 185, 204; of practitioners 49, 61
Addams, Jane 7
Advocacy 72, 117
Aging, adult education programs
for 116-118; advocate and
brokerage roles in helping
117; education of paraprofes-
sionals 117; essential economic concepts 112-115;
forecasts on welfare 114;
high school course content on
118-120; inadequate income
maintenance programs 115;
most pressing problems of
115; preparation for 111-112;
public education on aging
problems 112, 116
Aid to the Blind 98, 101
Aid to the Disabled 101
Aid to Families of Dependent
Children 101; and the courts
136-142; WIN Program 167
Aldrich, Gordon J. 31, 37
Alinsky, Saul 67, 70, 71, 72
Amenities 106
Anemia, hypochromic type
157, 165
Anomie 3, 44
Appelbaum, Richard P. 62, 110
Ares, Charles E. 128, 149, 151
Argersinger v. Hamlin, 130
Associated Charities 162, 164
Atomism 101

Bail practices, abuses 128-129;
and the Eighth Amendment
127; and the poor 127-128;
Federal Rules on Criminal
Procedure 128; Manhattan Project 147

Baker, Mary 84, 90
Batchelder, Alan B. 110
Behavior change 55, 60 (see
also Therapeutic interven-
tion)
Bendlich, Albert M. 151
Bennis, Warren 59
Bentham, Jeremy 100
Beveridge Commission 108
Bisno, Herbert 28, 58, 85, 90
Bloom, Martin 13, 35, 183-
184, 205
Boddie v. Connecticut 132
Boehm, Werner W. 11, 14,
20, 184
Borenzweig, Herman 10, 20
Borgotta, Edgar F. 83
Bracy, Joseph 63
Bureau of Federal Credit Un-
ions 117
Bureau of Labor Statistics 56;
moderate budget for a re-
tired couple 115; qualifica-
tions for urban helping ser-
vice professionals 51
Bureaucracy 69, 72
Burns, Eveline 9, 27, 47
Burns, Mary 27

Calvinism 96; punitive aspects
of 99, 100; stewardship and
99
Canada 58, 106
Capitalistic income distribution
45, 94, 112
Carleson v. Remillard 134
Categorical aid 105
Chadwick, George 206
Chambers, Clarke 10
Church controls 99
Churchman, C. West 198, 205
Cissell, Wayne 66

208

Intellectualism 100
Irving, Howard H. 47
Irwin, Justice Richard 129

Jackson, Justice 140-141
Jahns, Irwin 33, 37, 60, 82
James v. Valtierra 133, 141, 144
Johnston, Denis F. 181, 205
Jones, Wyatt G. 83
Juvenile justice system 123-127

Kadushin, Alfred J. 11, 21, 168, 184
Kahn, Alfred J. 11, 14, 21, 184
Katz, Carol H. 58
Katzenbach, Attorney General Nicolas, 146
Kendall, Katherine 28
Kennedy, Attorney General Robert 147
Kerr, John K. 114, 120
Killingsworth, Charles 75
Kilpatrick, James J. 171
Kincade, Robert G. 206
King, Donald W. 200, 206
King v. Smith 142, 143, 145
Knowledge and the helping function 4; essentials for brokerage role 19; in relation to values and skills 26; relative to social systems and agencies 29
Koff, Richard M. 204
Koprowski, Gene 28, 63, 84, 90
Kotz, Nick 109
Kramer, Ralph 110

Lanham Act 169
Law, and the poor 123, 146; definition 122; interpretation of civil liberty 142
Leakey, L. S. B. 76
Legal counsel and the poor 129-134; and civil cases 131; right to counsel 130, 135; right to remain silent 131; technical aid programs 131-132

Legal information 92, 93
Levitan, Sar A. 120
Lewis, Anthony 142, 150
Limited growth society 174; Club of Rome studies 174-181, 183; counter arguments 180

Maas, Henry S. 11, 14, 21, 184
McGee, Reece 62
McGrath, Earl J. 31, 37
Mack, Raymond 103, 110
McKiever v. Pennsylvania 125
McLean, Ann 23
McLeod, Donna L. 78
MacMahon, Brian 93
McPheeters, Harold L. 28, 37, 58, 85, 90
Macro-economic concepts 74, 75, 76
Malthus, Robert 100
Manpower 4, 106; in public service employment 106
Marcussen, Clifford 177
Marginality 3, 44
Marshall, Justice 138-140
Martin, John M. 124, 126, 149
Martindale, Don 46
Marx, Karl 51, 54, 103
Maslow hierarchy 187, 194
Mayer, Anna B. 172, 176
Meadows, Darella 179, 204
Means test 97, 98; uniformity in 105-107
Medicaid 163-164
Medical information 93; on Medicare 115
Medical needs of children in Florida, demographic data on sample 152; health complaints 157-159; immunization rates 154, 157, 158, 160-162; income differences 158; infant mortality rates 155; interview sample 157; interview schedule 154-155; intestinal parasites 162; racial differences 158; teeth 157-163
Mercantilism 99
Meyer, Carol 28

211

Roseman, Cyril 80
Ruderman, Floriance A. 178
Ruttan, Vernon W. 109

Samuelson, Paul 110
Scarpitti, Frank 10
Schon, Donald A. 51, 52, 61, 62, 64
Schuller, Lyle E. 80
Scott, W. Richard 62
Seeburger, Richard H. 149
Self identity 62
Shapiro v. Thompson 140, 144
Shick, Allen 53, 61
Silverman, Irving 47
Siporin, Max 10, 28, 85, 90
Sixth Amendment 125
Smith, Adam 41, 99
Smith, Charles U. 23
Smith, Gerald M. 62
Social brokerage 72 (see also Social work, and Roles of social workers)
Social change 3, 7, 42, 104; and day care needs 168; and the legal system 123; and occupational role shifts 7, 57; as an attribute of social organization 2, 51, 52; conflict and 51, 71, 103; functionalist and mechanistic views of 52; related to cybernetic technology 52; responses to 57; socio-cultural 52
Social Indicators 4, 185
Social organization 7; and disorganization 51, 53; dichotomies in description of 2; equilibrium theory and 43, 52; functionalist and mechanistic views of 2, 43
Social policy 68, 71, 102
Social problems 67, 82, 92, 179
Social science, common basic concepts 40; contributions of 5, 13, 18, anthropology 18, 76, 77, economics 18, 74, 76, political science 18, 72-74, sociology 18, 66; nature of 12, predictive potential,

27; relevance to social work 27; role in futuristic scenarios 182-183; use in approaching truth 1, 15
Social science applications, as regards educational objectives 11; barriers to incorporation of 11, 14, 30, 44, 184-185; communication problems 14, 44; cyclical history of interest in 10; dysfunctional integration systems 186; general approaches to 1; instructor preparation for 15, 33; need for 5; outlook in the 1970s 17; problems of incentives 33, 34; summary 65
Social Security Acts, impact of 1967 amendments 155; Noleo provision 136; public assistance as a right 144 (see also Suitable home laws)
Social systems, analysis of 5, 52, 72; and goals 55; awareness need 57; 117 basic functions of 3, 49; boundaries 3, change and 51; constraints 5; evaluation of 5, 42; helping service applications 5; hierarchies of 179; political science analysis 72, 73, 74; role of planning 182; reform of 56; value relationships 77
Social telesis 3
Social Welfare, definition 41; questions of scope 45; role of planning 41
Social Work, and challenges of change 60, 61; at BSW level 26; control functions of 13; evaluation of effectiveness 83, 84; job scarcities 26, 185; nature of 12; objectives of 85; prestige levels of 54, 56; social systems relationships 13
Social work education, and social change 60; generic focus 26; goals of 24; instructor qualifications 56; scholarship tradeoffs 187; social systems awareness problem 57

213